KEY
WOMEN
WRITERS
EDITOR SUE ROE

KATHERINE MANSFIELD

KEY
WOMEN
WRITERS
EDITOR : SUE ROE

KATHERINE MANSFIELD

KATE FULLBROOK

Senior Lecturer in English
Bristol Polytechnic

Indiana University Press
Bloomington and Indianapolis

Manufactured in Great Britain

Library of Congress Cataloging-in-Publication Data

Fullbrook, Kate.
    Katherine Mansfield.

    (Key women writers)
    Bibliography: p.
    1. Mansfield, Katherine, 1888–1923—Criticism
and interpretation. 2. Feminism and literature.
I. Title. II. Series.
PR9639.3.M258Z65   1986   823'.912   86-45392
ISBN 0-253-33161-7
ISBN 0-253-20401-1 (pbk.)

1 2 3 4 5 90 89 88 87 86

To Edward

Titles in the Key Women Writers Series

Key Women Writers
Series Editor: Sue Roe

The *Key Women Writers* series has developed in a spirit of challenge, exploration and interrogation. Looking again at the work of women writers with established places in the mainstream of the literary tradition, the series asks, in what ways can such writers be regarded as feminist? Does their status as canonical writers ignore the notion that there are ways of writing and thinking which are specific to women? Or is it the case that such writers have integrated within their writing a feminist perspective which so subtly maintains its place that these are writers who have, hitherto, been largely misread?

In answering these questions, each volume in the series is attentive to aspects of composition such as style and voice, as well as to the ideas and issues to emerge out of women's writing practice. For while recent developments in literary and feminist theory have played a significant part in the creation of the series, feminist theory represents no specific methodology, but rather an opportunity to broaden our range of responses to the issues of history, pyschology and gender which have always engaged women writers. A new and creative dynamics between a woman critic and her female subject has been made possible by recent developments in feminist theory, and the series seeks to reflect the important critical insights which have emerged out of this new, essentially feminist, style of engagement.

It is not always the case that literary theory can be directly transposed from its sources in other disciplines to the practice of reading writing by women. The series investigates the possibility that a distinction may need to be made between feminist politics and the literary criticism of women's writing which has not, up to now, been sufficiently emphasized. Feminist reading, as well as feminist writing, still needs to be constantly interpreted and re-interpreted. The complexity and range of choices implicit in this procedure are represented throughout the series. As works of criticism, all the volumes in the series represent wide-ranging and creative styles of discourse, seeking at all times to express the particular resonances and perspectives of individual women writers.

Sue Roe

Contents

Preface

Feminist literary criticism is, I believe, placing itself in grave danger. By definition, feminist criticism is grounded in a political commitment to claim the right of full and just appraisal for women's writing. It can claim certain recent successes, notably in the area of ex-huming women's writing from the oblivion to which it has largely been consigned by a male-dominated academic establishment. Understandably, at times, it has been marred by special pleading which is related to the political passion behind its production. But a different direction gives much more cause for unease. The linguistic and psychological fashions of the past ten years affirm rather than revise notions of sex and gender which disenfranchise women and their work. In adopting these ideas, feminist criticism, almost without noticing, is being subverted by a new sexist ideology.

Like other areas of literary criticism, recent feminist analysis has centred on a particular view of language. The structuralist project initiated by Saussure and Jakobson in the first part of the twentieth century, and which (along with its revisionist version, post-structuralism) threatens to dominate British and American literary criticism, continues the idealist, dualist tradition that has constrained western thought since the ancient Greeks. For the most part, this philosophical familiarity is the root of its attraction. Under the tyranny of dualism, where, to put it crudely, every positive must have its negative, it is fairly obvious that women must always lose. It is not only the case that women continue to be seen as 'body' to men's 'mind': the biological difference between men and women supports, as it always has supported for the dualist imagination, proliferating metaphors of capability and incapacity that lead directly to social and political results. In terms of the linguistic polarities presently exercising the critical imagination, if man is the 'speaker' – the active creator and enunciator of meaning – then women, by the 'law' of dualist opposition, must be passive, silent, incapable of utterance. Lévi-Strauss's description of the base of social order as a language of kinship systems which exist for the 'exchange' of women as commodities is a good example of the theoretical treatment of women within a structuralist programme. The *feminist* project, under such a metaphysical regime, can only hope to take one form – the creation of a new language, in words and in actions, a 'women's' language that will force the emergence of a new polarity. When such a process is imagined it is thought of as a way to mark out a separate, and this time *privileged* territory in which women can construct, and presumably impose, their own meanings. The wish is to trade new oppositions for old. Not only is this unlikely to happen, except in the most metaphorical way, but when one looks closely at the envisaged characteristics of the new 'ascendant' femininity, they look suspiciously like those of the old abased variety. Too much feminist criticism is caught in the same system of dualisms it needs to destroy.

If language is often defined as a male preserve that excludes women to the point that they are unable to speak even of their own condition, the territorial metaphor extends to include reason as a male stronghold. The recent interest in Lacan and his new Freudianism, for all its valuable attention to the split and decentred subject, places women where they have always been – that is, on the periphery of a phallocentric psychological paradigm which places language, logic and mental health in the domain of an all-powerful Father. For Lacan and his followers, the acquisition of language is the same as acquiescence to culture and to an identity already invented by culture. Both subjectivity and culture are contingent on accepting the power of traditional patriarchy as encoded in language. The family is still seen as the only important site for the production of the individual, and the Oedipal movement becomes the moment of acceptance of an historically-determined social order. Without such acceptance the individual – male or female – is excluded from speech and thus from humanity. For the boy, in Lacan's rereading of Freud's original theory, the resolution of the Oedipal complex means the surrender of the 'Imaginary', a polymorphous psychic realm which defies the rules of patriarchy. But this loss is compensated for by the promise of inclusion in the power of the Father. The girl, however, is left where she always has been abandoned by psychoanalysis – deprived, bereft, defined in terms of exclusion from power of all kinds except as the absent focal point for male fantasy. 'Women' is pure linguistic negation, unconsciousness, that which cannot be spoken. Lacan places women in silent polar opposition to a masculine domination that controls the course of culture and history.

The feminist thinker has some of the clearest historical reasons to distrust neat, polarised systems such as Lacan's. As Hannah Arendt argues in *The Origins of Totalitarianism*, it is the desire to see such simplistic binary intellectual systems established in political form that has caused the greatest cruelty and destruction in the world's history. Women, who have been victims of binary definitions for centuries, who have been a favourite target for idealist practice as well as idealist ideologies, are in a privileged position to affirm this danger. The rejection of essentialist and dualist definitions seems to me to be one of the most important tasks of the feminist critic, and one that has been often forgotten in recent years.

Literary feminism needs to be rooted in a non-essentialist base, and the practice of most of the best women writers has always been so grounded. The idea that even now is perhaps most startling for feminists and anti-feminists alike is the possibility that the sexes can not be categorised in any simple, schematic way, and that such schematisation is itself the basis of the varieties of sexist ideologies that have stifled women throughout history. As has often been noted without attention to its full implications, the history of women's oppression rests on selective attention to women's achievements and potentialities, especially those which violate preconceptions about gender. The feminist reader must be alert to avoiding such selectivity. For example, in literature, the narration of women's cultural consignment to silence and passivity is more than the refusal of the imposition of silence which it is usually taken to be. It is rather the destruction of silence, the *wreckage* of a traditional polarity between man as speaker and woman as mute. Writing of their condition is a strong and subversive part of women's history, and women have rarely been content to limit themselves to recording what the idealisms of their age have invented for them. For a feminist, attention to the ways women have constructed their own versions of meaning is of paramount importance as a surprisingly various corrective to a theoretical feminism which posits only a mirror-image of a sexist view of women's nature and history. In the following study of Katherine Mansfield, I shall attempt to avoid retrogressive theories that censor in advance ideas regarding what women might be.

Acknowledgements

My thanks to Sue Roe, Susan Manning, Ian Gordon, Richard Gravil, the librarians at the College of St Mark and St John, the English Faculty Library in Cambridge, the Cambridge University Library and the British Library, The Society of Authors as the literary representative of the Estate of Katherine Mansfield, and to Alfred A. Knopf, Inc. for permission to reprint excerpts from *Journal of Katherine Mansfield*, edited by John Middleton Murry (New York: Alfred A. Knopf, 1954), *Katherine Mansfield's Letters to John Middleton Murry*, 1913–1922, edited by John Middleton Murry (New York: Alfred A. Knopf, 1951), *The Letters of Katherine Mansfield*, edited by John Middleton Murry (New York: Alfred A. Knopf, 1929).

Introduction

Katherine Mansfield:
Reception and Reputation

Katherine Mansfield is one of the prose writers who,
along with Henry James, Gertrude Stein, James Joyce,
Virginia Woolf and Dorothy Richardson, is most
responsible for calling the twentieth-century reader into
being. It is a truism to say that modernist art, which
remains the most significant art of this era, developed
around two major concerns: a radically new sense of
human consciousness and a struggle to find a means of
literary expression adequate to convey the new ideas
about self, time and perception. The interests of the
modernist writers called for a new kind of prose – one
that devalued the linear progression of plot, that was
attuned to the image and the symbol, that developed
mood and voice as locations of meaning, and that
foregrounded a problematic investigation into the status
of the individual. In short, the interests of the writers
demanded the invention of a prose which called for *poetic*
reading, and which drew heavily on the traditional
devices of poetry for its articulation.

1

Katherine Mansfield transformed the short story in English, and she did so along significantly modernist lines. Her innovative writing was especially attuned to presentation of an unfixed and uncertain version of personality which was communicated through unifying images and through extraordinarily tight control of narration.[1] Her stories demanded a new kind of reader, and the aesthetic excitement with which her stories were first greeted registered this in a way that has generally been lost simply because the lessons of her writing have been so widely accepted. Katherine Mansfield is one of the major modernists and, along with Dorothy Richardson and Gertrude Stein, has had nothing like the serious attention that her writing demands.

Given the centrality of Katherine Mansfield's work to the shape of modern prose in English it is instructive to the feminist reader to consider the history of her literary reputation. It has exhibited all the signs of a textbook case of the devaluation of women's writing. The most concise and thoroughly representative summary of how Katherine Mansfield was to be seen already existed before her death. It occurs in D.H.Lawrence's *Women in Love* (1921) in which Katherine Mansfield has been fictionally transposed into the character of Gudrun. In a conversation between Rupert Birkin and Gerald Crich, Lawrence rehearses most of the points that were to become mainstays of Katherine Mansfield criticism. The exchange in question is about Gudrun's art, which is sculpture; Gerald Crich asks Birkin, the Lawrence figure, if her pieces are any good:

> 'I think sometimes they are marvellously good. That is hers, those two wagtails . . . you've seen them–they are carved in wood and painted.'

'I thought it was savage carving again.'

'No, hers. That's what they are–animals and birds, sometimes odd small people in everyday dress, really rather wonderful when they come off. They have a sort of funniness that is quite unconscious and subtle.'

'She might be a well-known artist one day?' mused Gerald.

'She might. But I think she won't. She drops her art if anything else catches her. Her contrariness prevents her taking it seriously – she must never be too serious, she feels she might give herself away. And she won't give herself away – she's always on the defensive. That's what I can't stand about her type.'[2]

The main points of Birkin's analysis need to be noted closely. He charges Gudrun with doing small things 'marvellously' well while being afraid to make the grand gesture, implying, ultimately, a fear of greatness, a refusal of 'seriousness', an acquiescence to minor status. The subjects of her art are always 'odd' and 'quaint'– marginal and unresponsive to history. Effects are gained subtly but unconsciously, without thought or direction. Finally, Gudrun is incapable of consistency in anything; her personality, which is simplistically linked with her work by Birkin, is in a constant state of flux that prevents full commitment to her art. She has a fear of both work and success, and the fault lies with 'her type', being, as she is, a woman who does not give herself away. The charge against Gudrun/Katherine Mansfield is that of running away from life as from art, despite a notable native talent for both.

Birkin's comments are, of course, 'fiction', but the elements in this particular passage match, point for point, the major notions which have informed Katherine Mansfield criticism. For the feminist reader Lawrence's critique is arresting in its open invocation of the most salient charges of sexist treatment of women's writing. Certain points – such as hints that 'small' works of art are necessarily inferior ones (a position that Lawrence as a poet and short-story writer could not himself have taken seriously), that women's art is bound to be 'homely' and domestic and therefore unimportant, and conversely, that women's art is 'savage', uncivilised – can be dismissed out of hand by the feminist critic. These are the kinds of view that have always trivialised women writers. They are examples of the type of preoccupation that confines Jane Austen to her famous 'little bit (two Inches wide) of Ivory' rather than registering her damning critique of her culture, or values Emily or Charlotte Brontë for their romantic, untutored 'wildness', rather than seeing the overall psychological precision of their works. Katherine Mansfield has been admired, indeed 'treasured', for the way in which many of her readers have conveniently seen her as fitting into these patterns.

In fact, Katherine Mansfield is an author whose life and work are particularly apt to elicit a number of prejudices. The most telling of these is a view of the woman artist (reflected at several points in Birkin's analysis of Gudrun) which is incapable of making anything but a naive correlation between the personality and the art of a woman. The prevalence of this view is one of the reasons that Katherine Mansfield's stories have been read, and read obsessively, as transparently 'confessional', complicated only by the fact that she was a complex character, a woman who did not 'give herself away'.[3] This particular fixation has led to Katherine Mansfield being read as a 'case' rather than as a writer – a development fostered by her husband, John Middleton Murry, who (sanctifying her after her early death) told the story of their life together on any occasion that could

bear it (and some that could not) for over thirty years.[4]
The deserved attention paid to Katherine Mansfield's
Journal and to her letters has also deflected interest away
from her art and onto her life. These factors led to the
creation of what can only be called a Katherine
Mansfield cult, soon followed by an anti-cult. For
members of both factions, as Sylvia Berkman noted in
1952, Katherine Mansfield was 'no longer a woman but
an enigmatic deity, half saint, half elf'.[5] While any
important author's life, especially one as dramatic as
Katherine Mansfield's, cannot help but attract attention, the problem for the assessment of her *as an artist* has
been the extent of this interest. Debates about her
writing have been displaced and invaded by debates of
another order. Was she sane? was she good? was she
'normal'? was she 'feminine'? are the questions which
most engage the majority of her critics.[6] The way in
which she analysed the world in a series of stories
written with exceptional lyricism and remarkable easy
subtlety is often slighted in the deflective activity of
finding 'the woman behind the work'. This again is a
common tactic for dealing with women writers. It allows
them to be neutralised – kept small, personal, confined to
the private life which has traditionally been the only life
any 'safe' woman may be presumed to lead.

It is not surprising that an author as subversive as
Katherine Mansfield should be read in this manner. It is ·
the way women writers have usually been read.
(Ironically, male writers, such as D.H.Lawrence himself,
who have been perceived, even temporarily, as challenging the status quo, and especially the sexual status quo,
are also likely to attract such treatment.) This kind of
reading is itself one of the specific difficulties that
women writers face simply because they are women.

The extent of these difficulties should never be

underestimated. As Simone de Beauvoir argues in *The Second Sex* (1949), women as authors are faced with problems that are directly related to the subjection of women in general. De Beauvoir clearly, and rather brutally, summarises these:

> Women do not contest the human situation, because they have hardly begun to assume it . . . they do not take the world incidentally, they do not ask it questions, they do not expose its contradictions: they take it as it is too seriously.[7]

De Beauvoir's assertion stems directly from her existential conception of freedom – one which Katherine Mansfield's work in many ways anticipates – an idea that posits the full and free assumption of the status of subject by the individual in a world that constantly threatens to reduce persons to the status of object. Women, because they are culturally defined as Other, in the light of male subjectivity, traditionally have not defined themselves but have been defined by others. Indeed, this is what being a woman has meant. It is the first lesson taught to all females: in de Beauvoir's famous phrase 'one is not born, but rather becomes, a woman' by accepting definition as object rather than seizing one's exigent individuality as subject. A 'feminine' sense of identity, therefore, traditionally has depended on the static nature of definitions accepted from outside the self; questioning the world is thus an activity that can lead to the destruction of the 'inauthentic' self, a self constructed not by the individual in any way but solely by the world that surrounds her. But inauthenticity, for de Beauvoir, is the greatest tragedy: it is the sacrifice of humanity itself. Women abandon whatever chance they have for freedom when they accept objectification, and as the world both lures and pushes them at every turn to accept this position, they have traditionally lived both falsely and without freedom. That is, they have lived in terms that deny the possibility of change.

However, de Beauvoir notes that throughout history, and within the modern period especially, another sort of woman is present: the independent woman who challenges cultural conventions that insist on women seeing themselves as objects to male subjectivity. These women are able to analyse for themselves the conditions of what it means to be defined as 'female'. De Beauvoir argues that while women in general and women writers in particular 'are still too preoccupied with clearly seeing the facts to try to penetrate the shadows beyond that illuminated circle', some women have given notable accounts of the 'circle' that encloses the world as it is. They

> make remarkable reporters. Women are able to describe atmosphere and characters, to indicate subtle relationships between the latter, to make us share in the secret stirrings of their souls. Willa Cather, Edith Wharton, Dorothy Parker, Katherine Mansfield, have clearly and sensitively evoked individuals, regions, civilisations.[8]

This clear understanding is necessary to get beyond what *is* to what *might be*. But few women, in de Beauvoir's opinion, have got beyond the reportorial stage as writers:

> We can count on the fingers of one hand the women who have traversed the given in search of its secret dimension: Emily Brontë has questioned death, Virginia Woolf life, and Katherine Mansfield – not very often – everyday contingence and suffering.[9]

Importantly, de Beauvoir tentatively identifies

Katherine Mansfield as one of a handful of women writers who have questioned the world. In her most successful stories Katherine Mansfield works precisely as de Beauvoir suggests. Her best fiction radically questions the forms and ideas that bind women, and men as well, into inauthentic lives. It is not therefore surprising that the darkness of her art is one of its hallmarks. While the surfaces of her stories often flash with sparkling detail, the underlying tones are sombre, threatening, and register the danger present in the most innocent seeming aspects of life.

It is only recently that critics have begun to sense the full force of the anger and of the direct cultural criticism displayed in Katherine Mansfield's work with regard to the condition of women. Elaine Showalter, for example, in *A Literature of Their Own*, reacts uneasily to the impact of the writing: 'Mansfield's fiction is cautionary and punitive; women are lured out onto the limbs of consciousness, which are then lopped off by the author.'[10] Showalter quotes with approval Virginia Woolf's 'disgust' with Katherine Mansfield's 'brutality', and Margaret Drabble's horror at the 'cruelty' of her characterisation. She repeats Lawrence's confounding of Katherine Mansfield's life and writing when she charges that 'the heroines of Katherine Mansfield's stories become the 'scapegoats' for her personal 'failures' '. Her worry is that Katherine Mansfield's vision of life, and women's lives in particular, is poisoned by a sense of failure, and that for the author 'the moment of self-awareness is also the moment of self-betrayal'.[11] Katherine Mansfield, she argues, sees

> women as artists whose creative energy has gone chiefly into the maintenance of myths about themselves and about those they love. To become aware of a myth is to lose faith

in it. Mansfield's characters are seen repeatedly at this moment of realisation and collapse.[12]

This is excellent analysis, and though it displeases Showalter, with her stated aim of searching for a positive and optimistic feminine tradition, it is precisely, as this study will argue, an aspect of Katherine Mansfield's writing that is profoundly successful. Katherine Mansfield sees the failure of many human relationships as grounded in a collaboration of victim and victimiser who are caught in a cycle of self-falsification that can only be broken by a confrontation of the bankruptcy of the terms of submission. The moment of realisation, in this context, *is* a moment of terror: ethical terror, and terror at the clash between the self that exists in the world in its masked and inauthentic form, and the vulnerable, confused and unstructured self beneath the mask. Oppression is thus contingent on the acceptance of a fixed identity and it is in acquiescing to such fixture that Katherine Mansfield, like de Beauvoir, believes that women have betrayed themselves most deeply. Through her exposure of the psychological base of oppression, Katherine Mansfield, in de Beauvoir's terms, both truly portrays the nature of objectification and reveals the secret mechanisms that support it. To refuse such writing on the grounds that it is 'brutal', or to dismiss it as 'miniaturist', or to bracket it off as 'mere' confessional, is to fail to understand the pressures against which anything that might legitimately be called freedom might be won, and to miss one of the main reasons for Katherine Mansfield's impact as a modernist writer.

Chapter One

Life, Letters and Journal

While any simple correlation between Katherine
Mansfield's personal life and her art must be rejected as a
sure way to falsify her literary production, it is also the
case that works of art do not exist in a timeless aesthetic
zone, free from history. The notion of the autonomous
aesthetic object has, for the time being, been removed
from the baggage of the literary critic. The idea of an
ahistorical art has been replaced by a view of literature
sensitive to the historical situation of both the writer
and of the reader. For a feminist critic this has generated
new opportunities for examining the kind of work
produced by women under the pressure of historical
circumstance.

The first revision that needs to be made by any literary
critic when approaching Katherine Mansfield is a change
in the general conception of modernism. The modernist
movement is usually portrayed as a largely male affair.
But it is not only the case that women writers had a
decisive effect on this literary revolution, it is also true

that one of the organising principles of the *avant-garde* writing of the period was centred on a new examination of gender, its origins and its instability. T. S. Eliot's Tiresias, Virginia Woolf's Lily Briscoe and Orlando, Joyce's Leopold Bloom and Katherine Mansfield's Kezia are all examples of this impulse working itself out. Once seen, this important aspect of modernism has clear links with contemporary debates about the nature of gender and with the continuing agitation by women to claim social and political rights. For women writers, there was, as Sydney Janet Kaplan argues, a 'vital link between experimentation and the need to express a definite sense of *women's* reality'.[1]

If women, as a caste, were struggling to reject the objectification that had been imposed on them there was a pressing need to find a new way of registering their experience and enunciating themselves as subjects. Further, women writers were analysing themselves with great attention to discover if, and if so *how*, they were other than they had been portrayed. Katherine Mansfield's 'confessional' writing needs to be read within this larger project. Her *Journal* and letters are more than the record of a brave, disordered and ridiculously short life. When this material is read as an extraordinarily various enactment of one woman's attempt to register her personal fight to build relationships unbounded by convention, to work out a new sense of the meaning of being a writer, and to resolve her passionate and constant engagement with problems of the nature of the self and of consciousness, it reveals itself as an important collection of documents in the history of women's self-awareness.

Katherine Mansfield's writing needs to be located within her personal history and the history of the age.

While her life has often been recounted, these accounts have almost always been skewed by blatant if undeclared biases and distortions. The bare outline of her biography, however, is easily drawn.[2] She was born Kathleen Mansfield Beauchamp in Wellington, New Zealand in 1888, the third daughter of an ambitious, second-generation colonial father who was to rise from poverty to a position of personal wealth and local power. Her mother was a vague figure who handed her children over to her own mother as they were born. Katherine Mansfield grew up in a household of women – her mother, her beloved grandmother, her mother's sister, and four Beauchamp daughters – which was dominated by a hyper-masculine father. The favoured child was the single son on whom the entire ménage doted.

From the time of her adolescence Katherine Mansfield was desperate to leave her family and New Zealand for Europe. She was sent with her sisters to a finishing school in London in 1903, and in 1908, already committed to being a writer, she persuaded her father to let her return to England with his blessing and an allowance that was to be her financial mainstay for the rest of her life.

The next year, her first of independence, was a disaster, and the available information about it is both tangled and unreliable. Katherine Mansfield seems to have become pregnant by a lover from New Zealand. She then married a man she scarcely knew and abandoned the marriage the next morning. Her mother travelled to England to investigate the marriage, found her daughter husbandless, sent her to Bavaria, and returned to New Zealand where she promptly cut Katherine Mansfield out of her will on the suspicion of lesbian tendencies. In Germany, Katherine Mansfield seems to have miscarried, but she also gathered the

13

material for her first collection of short stories, *In a German Pension*, which, when it was published in 1911, established her immediately as an important new writer. Her reputation was made and she became a fixture in literary and bohemian circles in London. Her vibrant but often troubled liaison with John Middleton Murry, whom she married in 1918, began in 1911.

The last decade of Katherine Mansfield's life, the period of her most successful writing, was a catalogue of disorder and difficulty. Murry's bankruptcy in 1912 made for continuing financial problems for himself and Katherine Mansfield; her personal death toll in World War I was staggering, not only was her brother killed, but, as Murry notes, 'no single one of Katherine's friends who went to the war returned alive from it.'[3] Katherine Mansfield was diagnosed as tubercular in 1917, well before the end of the war. The remainder of her life consisted of desperate and often excruciatingly lonely wanderings in search of health in the South of France, Italy and Switzerland, with painful dashes back to England to keep herself in contact with her friends and with Murry from whom she became progressively estranged. Her frantic attempts to write in the least settled circumstances and under the felt shadow of death only ended with her life. She died, in 1923, at the Gurdjieff Institute at Fontainebleu in a last-ditch attempt to find a spiritual miracle that would save her after the doctors had failed.

The details of Katherine Mansfield's life are almost unremittingly painful. As Claire Tomalin rightly says, the pattern of her life was 'both pathetic and almost ludicrously retributive; for every rash, false or wild thing she did she suffered a heavy punishment of the kind a Victorian novelist might have inflicted on an

erring heroine.'⁴ What is most remarkable about
Katherine Mansfield's *Journal* and letters is not an
obsession with the unplanned physical results of her
actions – undesired pregnancy, unwitting slip into addic-
tion to Veronal, undiagnosed venereal disease, tuberculosis – in fact, except for the fatal illness which demanded
her attention, these events scarcely figure in her
writing. They are not ignored but neither are they
treated as the defining secrets of a self perceived in
terms of transgression, punishment and atonement.
Instead, the *Journal*, a wide-ranging collection of observations, critical judgments, experiments and work in
progress, and the letters, which are as notable for their
shrewd, astringent intelligence as for their humour and
lyricism, leave the impression of vigour, freshness of
perception, playfulness and, most of all, of a tough-
minded inquiry into identity and art.

That this writing has generally been read as 'confessional' in quite another way is not surprising, and how it
has been read has a great deal to do with the fact that
Katherine Mansfield was a woman. In *The History of
Sexuality* Michel Foucault stresses the links between
confession and recognition of power in the choice of the
material which is confessed. He argues that in the
modern period sex has been transformed into the
primary confessional discourse with 'the confession that
truth and sex are joined, through the obligatory and
exhaustive expression of an individual secret' of sexual
desire being seen as the very heart of identity. 'What is
peculiar to modern societies,' writes Foucault, 'is not
that they consigned sex to a shadow existence, but that
they dedicated themselves to speaking of it *ad infinitum*,
while exploiting it as *the* secret.'⁵ The 'sexualisation' of
confession within this period, and the transfer of the
power of confessor from the Church to a new medical

priesthood has especially far-ranging effects on women. It has secured again the ideological bonds that lock her into the structure of the family which is prescribed as the only safe location for the containment of female desire. And it has further convinced both men and women to continue to 'problematise' women exclusively in terms of biological sexuality.

Katherine Mansfield's interest in identity follows a different course. While questions of gender were of importance to her (it could scarcely be otherwise), she refused to privilege sexuality as the unifying principle of consciousness. She understood the pressure to restrict self to sexual determinants and the *Journal* and letters record her constant rejection of this ideology. For this reason she often mocked the fashion for psychoanalysis in fiction,[6] and a letter of 1916 announces her categorical refusal of the sexualisation of perception: '*I shall never* see sex in trees, sex in the running brooks, sex in the stones and sex in everything.'[7]

The ideas that underlie Katherine Mansfield's own statements about consciousness and identity need to be seen in terms of the symbolist theory of the mask.[8] It is a point of reference which deeply affects Katherine Mansfield's fiction and also helps to explain what she repeatedly defined in her *Journal* as her 'philosophy–the defeat of the personal'.[9] In its basic form the idea of the mask is not new. One can look to the Greeks or, like Yeats, to the Japanese Noh theatre to find artistic expression of the masked extinguishing of individual character treated as a metaphor for the human condition in the drama. More important for Katherine Mansfield was the example of the Decadents of the 1890s whose characteristic *doppelgänger* theme was built on the idea of an artificially constructed self that overlay an uncontrollable *alter ego*. Katherine Mansfield was an early and avid reader of Oscar Wilde, a major source of symbolist ideas for readers in English, and she accepted many of Wilde's ideas about the self and extended them. The result was that she questioned the notion of a stable self which could be 'lost' under the detritus of social forms, but which nevertheless existed in a pure and discoverable state within the depths of individual being. Instead, she conceived of self as multiple, shifting, non-consecutive, without essence, and perhaps unknowable. The extreme vulnerability of identity under such a conception is at the centre of her view of character. The only protection for individuals, who are in constant danger of utter fragmentation, is the covering of a mask, a consciously wrought presentation of a coherent self that was of necessity artificial. Her warning to Murry–'Don't lower your mask before you have another mask prepared beneath, as terrible as you like – but a mask'[10] – emphasises her sense of the individual's dependence on a mask for survival.

The understanding of the complete isolation of the individual, both from others and from any sure sense of self, that follows from such a theory has a decisive effect on a number of recurring aspects of Katherine Mansfield's writing. Her pessimism, her sense of fixed social forms as laughably flimsy and arbitrary and yet powerful as the sources of an otherwise unattainable communal illusion of certainty about individuals, and the sudden shifts in tone that emphasise discontinuity of vision are all, in their different ways, related to her ideas regarding the self. One finds, particularly in the *Journal*, a constant strain to keep these ideas clear. This tension is generated by another facet of Katherine Mansfield's legacy from the symbolists; that is, an attraction to a mystic notion of an essential self, discoverable only in moments of spiritual inspiration. This second strand of thought related to identity and consciousness often prompts in Katherine Mansfield what can only be called a philosophical nostalgia for a guarantee against complete isolation in the world. And these two, contradictory ideas, often simultaneously present, sometimes elicits writing that is a powerful evocation of a central dilemma of the age. For example, a journal entry from 1920, on the recurrence of Polonius's advice to Hamlet in old-fashioned autograph albums is shaped by this tension. "'To thine own self be true",' Katherine Mansfield writes,

> True to oneself! which self? Which of my many–well, really, that's what it looks like coming to–hundreds of selves? For what with complexes and repressions and reactions and vibrations and reflections, there are moments when I feel I am nothing but the small clerk of some hotel without a proprietor, who has all his work cut out to enter the names and hand the keys to the wilful guests.
>
> Nevertheless, there are signs that we are intent as never before on trying to puzzle out, to live by, our own particular self. *Der Mensch muss frei sein*–free distangled, single. Is it not possible that the rage for confession, autobiography, especially for memories of earliest childhood, is explained by our persistent yet mysterious belief in a self which is continuous and permanent; which, untouched by all we acquire and all we shed, pushes a green spear through the dead leaves and through the mould, thrusts a scaled bud through years of darkness, until, one day, the light discovers it and shakes the flower free – and we are alive – we are flowering for our moment upon the earth? This is the moment which, after all, we live for, – the moment of direct feeling when we are most ourselves and least personal.[11]

The exasperated, jokey tone of the first part of the passage, which is dominated by a sophisticated, brittle stoicism that Katherine Mansfield and Dorothy Parker equally cultivated and which is now the most immediately recognisable tone of the 1920s, is completely dropped in the second, lyrical part of the passage with its organic, romantic, mystic vocabulary. The passage is extremely telling. It enacts Katherine Mansfield's knowledge of the divergence of her ideas about the self as much in its shift of metaphors as in its discourse. But it also enacts Katherine Mansfield's deep but resisted desire to believe in a continuous self that holds the possibility of release from roles, masks and fragmentation into a moment of pure being. Katherine Mansfield *almost* subscribes to the Bergsonian ideas common among other modernist writers – in what Joyce called 'epiphanies' and Virgina Woolf 'moments of being'. But while she is attracted to the possibility of a unified self, even if knowable only in infinitesimal moments, there is a final hanging back. And it is this hesitation, this honest uncertainty in the face of desire and need, that finally makes Katherine Mansfield, at times, one of the toughest and darkest of the modernists.

The need itself pushes her to explore every possible discoverable aspect of self, and to distrust, as well as record, every movement of consciousness she could force into language. Like Virginia Woolf (and both women were aware of the similarities in their writing)[12] the evanescence and power of the sea becomes Katherine Mansfield's most common metaphor for consciousness, its cruelty and its mystery. In another journal entry in 1920 she records her sense of the inadequacy of language to give an account of consciousness, as well as, again, the tension between the two rival views of self:

And yet one has these 'glimpses', before which all that one ever has written (what has one written?) – all (yes, all) that one ever had read, pales ... The waves, as I drove home this

19

afternoon, and the high foam, how it was suspended in the air before it fell . . . What is it that happens in that moment of suspension? . . .

I don't want to be sentimental. But while one hangs, suspended in the air, held, – while I watched the spray, I was conscious *for* life of the white sky with a web of torn grey over it; of the slipping, sliding, slithering sea; of the dark woods blotted against the cape; of the flowers on the tree I was passing; and more – of a huge cavern where my selves (who were like ancient sea-weed gatherers) mumbled, indifferent and intimate . . . and this other self apart in the carriage . . . Shall one ever be at peace with oneself?[13]

For Katherine Mansfield, then, the writer works on the razor's edge between despair and discovery, between the possibility of complete isolation and the possibility of mystic penetration of the world. Katherine Mansfield's awareness of the implications of these contradictory ideas only grew slowly, and she never fully resolved the contradiction, though the *Journal* and letters both move gradually towards a spiritualised view of the artist with a special status as truth-teller. In her insistence on the moral elevation of the artist Katherine Mansfield's late writing places her in the central tradition in English criticism that runs from Coleridge and Shelley through Matthew Arnold and Wilde and into the twentieth century. But from the beginning, the grounds on which she claimed a privileged place for the artist was that of liberation from social restraint, and the right, indeed the duty, of the artist to push experience to its limits. The opening of the *Journal*, in particular, is a confident declaration of revolt against the conditions that threatened to enclose her. As early as 1906 Katherine Mansfield was transcribing Wilde's aphorisms with enthusiasm: ' "No life is spoiled but one whose growth is arrested" '; ' "Push everything as far as it will go." '[14] The sheer aggressive exuberance of the first part of the *Journal*, with its confident belief in 'genius' and its scoffing at fear, marks her early rejection of what she saw as the unreal and undesirable security of her colonial background (though Katherine Mansfield transposes its resources of brashness, self-confidence and privilege to the artistic sphere).

From the start, too, she saw women as subject to special dangers, inimical to their development, which she was determined to avoid. While quoting Wilde, she also cites the journal of the painter, Marie Bashkirtseff: *'"Me marier et avoir des enfants! Mais quelle blanchisseuse–je veux la gloire."'* 'La gloire' was also what the young Katherine Mansfield was after, as she tried to understand her self and its 'thousand million lives' and planned to 'write something so beautiful, and yet modern'.[15] Her reaction to Elizabeth Robbins's *Come and Find Me* in 1908 is a clear indication of how shrewdly she comprehended the situation of women, and how self-assured she was about her own capability to escape it:

> Really, a clever, splendid book; it creates in me such a sense of power. I feel that I do now realise, dimly, what women in the future will be capable of. They truly as yet have never had their chance. Talk of our enlightened days and our emancipated country – pure nonsense! We are firmly held with the self-fashioned chains of slavery. Yes, now I see that they *are* self-fashioned and must be self-removed . . . . Independence, resolve, firm purpose, and the gift of discrimination, *mental clearness* – here are the inevitables. Again, Will – the realisation that Art is absolutely self-development. The knowledge that genius is dormant in every soul – that that very individuality which is at the root of our being is what matters so poignantly.
>
> Here then is a little summary of what I need – power, wealth and freedom. It is the hopelessly insipid doctrine

that love is the only thing in the world, taught, hammered into women, from generation to generation, which hampers us so cruelly. We must get rid of that bogey – and then comes the opportunity of happiness and freedom.[16]

Although, as has already been seen, Katherine Mansfield developed an uneasiness about the romantic vocabulary of the self that she so confidently uses here, and although she also shifted her ideas of art away from the personal, this early statement indicates her clear understanding of the mental effects of the social subordination of women that is a constant concern in her fiction. Katherine Mansfield's feminism came as a matter of course, so much so that overt discussion of it as a political principle is absent from her writing while its underlying presence is everywhere.

If Katherine Mansfield was determined to push herself outside the boundaries drawn for women of her era and class, she was often unwillingly caught by the very circumstances she despised. Gender roles are not easily dissolved, and especially in her relationship with Murry, stereotyped expectations seem to have been a constant source of internal and external friction that forced Katherine Mansfield into classic female impasses and which elicited writing that can be regarded as equally classic women's laments. A letter of 1913 is a good example; it oscillates between complaint, pro-pitiation and rage, makes charges of unfair treatment, and retreats behind the barriers of social hierarchies:

Am I such a tyrant, Jack dear – or do you say it mainly to tease me? I suppose I'm a bad manager, and the house seems to take up so much time if it isn't looked after with some sort of method. I mean ... when I have to clear up twice over or wash up unnecessary things I get frightfully impatient and want to be working. So often this week, I've heard you and Gordon talking while I washed the dishes. Well, someone's got to wash dishes and get food. Otherwise – 'there's nothing in the house but eggs to eat.' Yes, I hate *hate* doing these things that you accept just as all men accept of their women. I can only play the servant with very bad grace indeed. It's all very well for females who have nothing to do . . . and then you say I am a tyrant and wonder why I get tired at night! . . . – and Monday after you and Gordon and Lesley have gone I walk about with a mind full of ghosts of saucepans and primus stoves and 'Will there be enough to go round?' . . . and you calling (whatever I am doing) '*Tig,* isn't there going to be tea? It's five o'clock,' as though I were a dilatory housemaid.[17]

The mask that Katherine Mansfield herself wore as Murry's wife became increasingly difficult to support as time went on, and almost impossible during the final years of her illness. An attempt in the *Journal* of 1921 to think out an ideal relationship between men and women was quickly written off as a failure:

We are neither male nor female. We are a compound of both. I choose the male who will develop and expand the male in me; he chooses me to expand the female in him. Being made 'whole'. . . . And why I choose *one* man for this rather than many is for safety. We bind ourselves within a ring and that ring is as it were a wall against the outside world. It is our refuge, our shelter. Here the tricks of life will not be played. Here is safety for us to grow.[18]

But this comforting, protective androgyny, while theoretically possible for her, in no way fit her experience: Katherine Mansfield pulls herself up – '*Why* I *talk like a child!*' The dream of finding a safe haven in marriage from the danger of the world is rejected as invalid. For the most part of the late *Journal* and the late letters record more and more a sense of isolation; the only satisfaction that Katherine Mansfield found was in her work, which became increasingly important to her.

Art, she thought, was beyond sex or gender and involved a leap into another order of experience, although its *purpose* was to report on the detail of apprehended life. She always referred to the artist in universal terms, and this was progressively emphasised as she moved from the overt social criticism of the early writing to the more subterranean but also more intense protest of her later work. This shift is evident in Katherine Mansfield's *Journal* and letters where her discussion of the artist revolves increasingly around the idea of the expression of the interpenetration of being. In accordance with the aesthetic ideas of the time she looked for a principle and a technique that would pull together consciousness and the external world. In a letter to S.S.Koteliansky in 1915 she asks:

> Do you, too, feel an infinite delight and value in *detail* – not for the sake of detail but for the life *in* the life of it. . . . do you ever feel as though the Lord threw you into Eternity – into the very exact centre of eternity, and even as you plunge you felt every ripple floating out from your plunging – every single ripple floating away and touching and drawing into its circle every slightest thing that it touched.[19]

Katherine Mansfield was looking, in short, for a way out of the socially-constructed self. The fullest expression of what she attempted to do in her writing is given to Dorothy Brett in a letter of 1917:

> It seems to me so extraordinarily right that you should be painting Still Lives just now. What can one do, faced with this wonderful tumble of round bright fruits; but gather them and play with them – and *become them*, as it were.When I

pass an apple stall I cannot help stopping and staring until I
feel that I, myself, am changing into an apple, too, and that
at any moment I can produce an apple, miraculously, out of
my own being . . . . When you paint apples do you feel that
your breasts and your knees become apples too? Or do you
think this is the greatest nonsense. I don't . . . . When I write
about ducks I swear that I am a white duck with a round eye,
floating on a pond fringed with yellow-blobs and taking an
occasional dart at the other duck with the round eye, which
floats upside down beneath me . . . . In fact the whole
process of becoming the duck . . . is so thrilling that I can
hardly breathe, only to think about it. For although that is
as far as most people can get, it is really only the 'prelude'.
There follows the moment when you are *more* duck, *more*
apple, or *more* Natasha than any of these objects could ever
possibly be, and so you *create* them anew . . . that is why I
believe in technique . . . because I don't see how art is going
to make that divine *spring* into the bounding outline of
things if it hasn't passed through the process of trying to
become these things before re-creating them.[20]

This may seem very far from consideration of
Katherine Mansfield as a woman writer, but I think in
fact it is not. The escape from self into the apple or the
duck or eternity which Katherine Mansfield describes
with such passion, is an escape from a *specific* if not
completely knowable self. It is an aesthetic that
concentrates on the removal of limitation from the
individual and part of that limitation (and one she
concentrates on in her stories) is that of gender. What
Katherine Mansfield claims for the artist, whether male
or female, is the possibility of the conscious application
of intention to shape and change the contents of
consciousness. And the way out of self, for Katherine
Mansfield, was specifically technique, that is, the
invention of a new way of speaking, a new way of
ordering the reportage of perception that encoded a

change in the nature of perception itself by enunciating a change in what could be perceived. The artist, by so working, demonstrates and enacts the power of consciousness to change history.

This is what Katherine Mansfield was referring to in her letters in 1921 when she insisted that 'life and work are two things indivisible. It's only by being true to life that I can be true to art'.[21] And, in another letter:

> It seems to me like this. Here is painting and here is life – we can't separate them. Both of them have suffered an upheaval extraordinary in the last few years. There is a kind of tremendous agitation going on still, but so far anything that has come to the surface seems to have been experimental, or a fluke – a lucky accident. I believe the only way to *live* as artists under these new conditions in art and life is to put everything to the test for ourselves. We've got, in the long run, to be our own teachers . . . . I think if artists were really thorough and honest they would save the world. It's the lack of those things and the reverse of them that are putting a deadly blight on life. Good work takes upon it a Life – bad work has death in it.[22]

Critics have often related Katherine Mansfield's developing faith in the power of art to transform the world and her strenuous view of the work of the artist to her growing disconnection from life in her last years as illness cut her off from almost all other kinds of activity. But this reading ignores the fact that writers as diverse as Henry James and Wyndham Lewis who did not suffer from such restrictions, but who, as men, might be expected to live the intellectual life rather than the 'female' life of satisfaction via emotional relationships, thought very much the same thing. One must not dismiss Katherine Mansfield's ideas on such suspicious grounds. And it must be further noted that in formulating such an aesthetic Katherine Mansfield again stressed the artist's immersion in history as being of cardinal significance.

The writer, for Katherine Mansfield, was reponsible to history or was nothing. As she writes in a letter, again in 1921, to Sydney Schiff:

> The artist who denies his Time, who runs away from it even so much as the fraction of a hair is false. First he must be free; that is, he must be controlled by none other than his deepest self, his truest self. And then he must accept Life, he must submit – give himself so utterly to Life that no personal *quâ* personal self remains.[23]

The repeated emphasis on extinguishing the personal points to Katherine Mansfield's belief in the role of the artist as a prime agent in the communal transformation of sensibilities. What she had in mind might be more easily understood in the light of some of her comments on the effects she believed the historical trauma of World War I should have on fiction.

While the war was in progress Katherine Mansfield rarely mentioned it in her writing except on the several occasions when she was personally caught on the fringes of the conflict. But, writing to Murry in 1919 while reviewing Virginia Woolf's *Night and Day*, she declares her unease with the contemporary novel in general because, she felt, it turned its back on the war and slid into forms and usages that simply deleted recent history:

> My private opinion is that it is a lie in the soul. The war never has been: that is what the message is. I don't want (G. forbid!) mobilization and the violation of Belgium, but the novel can't just leave the war out . . . . I feel in the *profoundest* sense that nothing can ever be the same – that, as artists, we are traitors if we feel otherwise: we have to take it into

account and find new expressions, new moulds for our new thoughts and feelings . . . . We have to face our war.[24]

A few days later she returns to the subject and to her disgust with the post-war novel for failing to respond to history:

> . . . the more I read the more I feel all these novels will not do . . . I can't imagine how after the war these men can pick up the old threads as though it had never been. Speaking to you I'd say we have died and live again. How can that be the same life? . . . In a way it's a tragic knowledge; it's as though, even while we live again, we face death. But *through Life*: that's the point.[25]

What Katherine Mansfield had in mind for the writer as an appropriate response to history was not, as her sarcastic comment about 'mobilization and the violation of Belgium' indicates, realist documentary, but rather the expression and therefore realisation of the transformation of consciousness. A note on Hegel in the *Journal* emphasises this point:

> Art is not the attempt of the artist to reconcile existence with his vision; it is an attempt to create his own world *in* this world. That which suggests the subject to the artist is the *unlikeness* to what we accept as reality. We single out – we bring into the light – we put up higher.[26]

Katherine Mansfield once reflected that 'It is pleasant to plant cuttings of futurity if only one in ten takes root.'[27] The writer, for her, *makes* the future into something other than the past: writing, for Katherine Mansfield, is a means for the transformation of the world. It is, in a fundamental sense, a mode of revolution.

Katherine Mansfield's *Journal* and letters contain a

coherent account of the ideas on which her fictional practice is based, and in focusing on this material other aspects of the writing necessarily have been neglected. But it would be unjust to her writing to leave its extraordinary variousness unnoticed. The letters are fascinating for the range of personae that Katherine Mansfield manufactures for her correspondents. In all this writing the diversity and control of emotional tone is remarkable. The writing is alternately sensuous or cynical, sarcastic or whimsical, deadly earnest or absurdist. Then there is her equally extraordinary originality of perception: there are things one feels she is the first to record, like the following precise account of a certain type of gluttony.

> L.M. is also exceedingly fond of bananas. But she eats them so slowly, so terribly slowly. And they know it – somehow; they realise what is in store for them when she reaches out her hand. I have seen bananas turn absolutely livid with terror on her plate – or pale as ashes.[28]

Her critical reactions to other authors is often similarly economic, irreverent and acute. For example, she notes of E.M.Forster's *Howard's End* that, 'it's not good enough. E.M.Forster never gets any further than warming the teapot. Is it not beautifully warm? Yes, but there ain't going to be no tea.'[29] There are powerful vignettes drawn from everyday observations – a cat refuses a dead mouse, a woman eats a strawberry, a dog is given a bone, a gardener proves himself a petty swindler – that become luminous symbols for the whole areas of human experience.

In 'Some Notes Defining a "Feminist Literary Criticism"', Annette Kolodny writes of the tendency to dismiss women's autobiographical writing as other than intentional so that 'the inherently sexist view might be maintained that women's productions are attributable to something less than fully conscious artistic invention.[30] Katherine Mansfield's 'confessional' writing, attuned to history, consciousness, identity and observation, and written with the same precision that characterises her fiction, demonstrates the inadequacy of that view.

Chapter Two

The Early Stories

If Katherine Mansfield's idea of the artist transcended both sex and gender, her fiction is nevertheless focused on enactments of the roles of men and women; it trains a clear intelligence on the psychological effects of gender barriers and enclosure. Her theoretical idea of the artist allowed her the sense of distance, and, indeed, estrangement from those sexual constructions that she needed in order to devise fictions in which her characters' identities are riddled with gender codes as if with an unshakeable disease. This may sound like overstatement, but close scrutiny of the stories reveals Katherine Mansfield's continual, even obsessive attention to the defining and distorting part that gender plays in the relationships between individuals and in shaping society.

It is often said that fiction concerns itself most closely with manners and morals. It would be better to say that the history of fiction is *part* of the history of manners and morals in that it is one major way to codify and enact in language the ethical judgements that are features of a given time and place. As moralist, the artist often serves as a kind of outlaw, not only recording the dominant values of his or her culture, but pushing beyond the compromise of typical pratice by dramatising hypothetical moral codes, or, by dramatising what the world would look like if the stated values of the culture were substituted for hidden codes which actually determine behaviour but which are left, at least partially, unspoken. Thus hypocrisy, double-dealing – the 'textual corruption' that falsifies the area between the theory and practice of ethical codes – is often precisely the subject that lies at the core of the rebellious author's work.

Katherine Mansfield is one of these rebels, and the central characters in her fiction are often themselves outlaws. But they are outlaws of a particular kind; their rebelliousness does not lie so much in overt gestures as in processes of the mind and in the moments that crystallise out of consciousness to reveal to them the discrepancies between their underlying natures and the fixed social masks which they, often confidently, wear. This is not the kind of fiction in which heroic individuals pit themselves against an obviously unjust society, but a fiction in which the individual discovers herself as socially constructed, or is revealed to the reader as socially constructed, and yet possessed of previously unrecognised and unregarded elements of consciousness whose very presence indicates the potential difference of the self from how it has been perceived. The radical incompleteness and selectivity of social definition is thereby revealed.

To emphasise the discontinuity of these moments of truly existential wonder and terror, Katherine Mansfield, sharing in the central modernist impulse in relation to the formal structuring of fiction, moved further and further away from plot as the organising principle in her writing. As Clare Hanson notes in *Short Stories and Short Fictions, 1880–1980*, both the view of causal relations embodied in the conventional plot and the neat 'finality' of the traditional ending seemed, for the modernists in general and Katherine Mansfield in particular, 'to convey the misleading notion of something finished, absolute, and wholly understood'.[1] Katherine Mansfield's ideas ran counter to those that stood behind the shape of the traditional short story. However, although she always hoped to write a novel, she chose the short-story form itself as the most appropriate vehicle for the expression of this view of the world. For, as Hanson again rightly argues, the short story, like the short and fragmented poetry also typical of the period, formally suited the modernist view of the discovery of meaning and of the self – brief, unpredictable, discontinuous, tied in no orderly way to rational or sequential experience.

But, by necessity, art is the imposing of order on what may appear (indeed, what may *be*) amorphous and formless. The modernists still needed a basis of order to replace the comforting linearity of plot. The solution was to follow the late nineteenth-century symbolist lead into adopting the logic of the image and of the symbol as the means for formal unification of their work. That Katherine Mansfield herself did so must be seen as part of what she was attempting to say in her fiction. As Pierre Macherey insists, any 'project of writing begins inevitably by taking the form of an ideological imperative – something to *say.*' The problem for the writer

is not that of being restricted by rules – or the absence of such a restriction – but the necessity of inventing forms, or forms derived from a principle which transcends the enterprise itself, but forms which can be used immediately

33

as the means of expression of a determinate content; likewise the question of the value of these forms cannot reach beyond the immediate issue.

Form, Macherey goes on to argue 'takes the shape or changes in response to a new imperative of the idea.'[2] The 'imperatives' behind Katherine Mansfield's fiction can be enumerated as the rejection of traditional accounts of the unified self, the need to expose their inadequacy, a special urge to record the damage that these accounts had done to women, and the desire to explore the possibilities that a new view of the self might mean for the transformation of individuals. The forms that Katherine Mansfield uses in her short stories are constantly straining to enact these ideas.

Katherine Mansfield evolved for these uses a story form whose surface is deceptively clear but whose images signal crises for the individual which are in fact crises for the entirety of the ideological fabric that holds the individual in her masked place. The only way to read such stories, to 'get at' them, is to be alert to their obliqueness, untrustworthy surfaces, and lack of overt narrative instruction for the reader at the same time as paying attention to the urgent signs of meaning that are dissolved all through the text rather than being concentrated at climactic points. The method itself is a part of the commentary on the world that sees experience as not easily readable but difficult, obscure, and very likely to be other than it seems.

From all this it should be obvious what Katherine Mansfield's technique has to do with her presentation of women. If the traditional view of women is that they should be, in several senses of the word, 'selfless', yet at the same time completely enclosed by strict social definitions, the implications of Katherine Mansfield's ideas of the self blow any fixed notion of 'women' to pieces. Gender at once becomes an elaborate joke and an obviously *invented* prison. Katherine Mansfield both charts the dimensions of this prison and considers ways to dismantle it. The fiction repeatedly circles around a number of questions relating to women: What does it mean to be defined as female? What does such definition do to the way women experience themselves and the world? Is an alternative definition possible and what might it be like? How is the girl-child tamed into womanhood? And, most importantly, what does it feel like to be a woman alone; what happens to a 'relative creature' when there is no one to be relative to?

'I do believe,' Katherine Mansfield wrote to Ottoline Morrell in 1919, 'that the time has come for a "new word" but I imagine that the new word will not be spoken easily. People have never explored the lovely medium of prose. It is a hidden country still – I feel that so profoundly.'[3] Katherine Mansfield's own evolution of a 'new word' for the short story was accomplished in a remarkably short period of time. There are less than fourteen years between her first important story, 'The Tiredness of Rosabel', which she wrote in 1908 when she was nineteen, and her last, 'The Canary', in 1922. While Katherine Mansfield's method was not fully developed until the completion of 'Prelude', which she worked on from 1915 to 1917, her early fiction has its own intrinsic interest, both as an initial statement of what were to become her most characteristic concerns, and for the success of some of the writing. The early fiction is both more overtly aggressive and more obviously politically embattled than the later work. Very broad satire is favoured and a utopian impulse underlies many of the stories. A keen eye for injustice and a profound feeling for the isolation of individuals inform these stories that swing between Chekhovian realism and the modes of the parable or the fable.

'The Tiredness of Rosabel' marks the start of Katherine Mansfield's mature writing. Although it was composed in 1908 it was not published until 1924 in the posthumous volume, *Something Childish*, which included many of Katherine Mansfield's previously uncollected early stories. The subject is a crucial one for feminist writers – the contrast between the material conditions and the dream life of a working girl. In the story, Katherine Mansfield works the same ground as that in . Henry James's fine *nouvelle* of 1898, *In the Cage*, uncovering the fantasies that support and make tolerable the otherwise crushing conditions of exploitation which entrap the girl. Katherine Mansfield stresses the connection between the economic function of her tired Rosabel, a milliner at the end of a long day, and her daydreams which pathetically uphold the whole sexual and social structure that degrades her.

The story begins with an account of Rosabel's return from the shop to her sad fourth-floor room. The girl, for all the expendable anonymity of her position in society, has a hunger for beauty for which she pays heavily – she buys a bunch of violets in spite of only being left with enough money for a meagre tea. As she drags through London on her way home, the city is presented in two series of images, both representing the girl's perceptions. The first series stresses crowding, ugliness and dirt, and is summed up by a description of Rosabel's wet feet, and her skirt and petticoat's coating of 'black greasy mud'. The other is a function of the girl's consciousness too, which oscillates between her unhealthy lack of basic material needs (her first daydream is of food: 'roast duck and green peas, chestnut stuffing, pudding with brandy sauce') and her lack of excitement, pleasure and beauty. Rosabel's mind provides her with what is palpably not there to satisfy her in the physical world. She interprets the scene she sees through the steamed windows of a crowded bus as magical: everything seem 'blurred and misty, but light striking on the panes turned their dullness to opal and silver, and the jewellers' shops seen through this, were fairy palaces.'4 What is important here is Rosabel's consciousness as she infuses the wet city with the glamour that satisfies her craving for something other than the life she actually leads.

Katherine Mansfield picks up the symbol of the violets and meshes it with a typical incident in the milliner's working day for the central daydream of the story. The handsome, rich young couple that Rosabel has waited on during the day becomes a starting-point for her tired, slightly feverish fantasies. She imagines herself changing places with the rich woman; the handsome young man brings her masses of Parma violets, feeds her luxuriously, keeps her warm, dry, loves her, marries her. Katherine Mansfield inserts a brilliantly placed aside into the daydream at the moment of sexual surrender – '(The real Rosabel, the girl crouched on the floor in the dark, laughed aloud and put her hand up to her hot mouth).'5 Having drawn her emotional sustenance from her dream, Rosabel pulls her grimy quilt around her neck and goes to sleep, waking only to smile as she shivers in the 'grey light' of dawn in the 'dull room'.

The intersection of the daydream's comforts with Rosabel's real needs makes the fantasy more than a condescending excursion into the clichés of 'silver-spoon' romance, though the fact that Katherine Mansfield used these clichés to populate her character's mind is itself as much her comment on the power of entrenched imaginative forms to control the contents of consciousness as it is an attack on the final cruelty of such images as drugs for the minds of oppressed women.

The young Katherine Mansfield recognised the *function* of trash romance for women (whose elements have not significantly changed), which invites dreams of being the perfect beneficiaries of the sexual system that in fact victimises them. Rosabel is part of a complex social system in which she works and suffers so that rich women may catch their rich men. But there are other impulses revealed as well. Rosabel's need for beauty in her life is as real to her as her need for food. The crudities of her daydream are the semi-conscious expression of needs that are reflected in buying the violets and in her vision of the opalescent city for which there is no outlet for her except in dreams. The discontinuity between what Rosabel 'knows' at one level and what she 'dreams of' on another level of her consciousness is, as much as the wet clothes and lack of food, part of the reason for the fever, the slight hysteria that the narrator implies is the representative state of the trapped working girl, 'the girl crouched on the floor in the dark'. The inaccessibility of the meaning of the story, with its two disparate sets of images that only the reader can pull together, to the consciousness of the central character forms a crucial aspect of the story's meaning. It marks Katherine Mansfield's engagement from the first with experimental narration as part of her commitment to speak truly of the lives of women.

The theme of exploitation of women, along with the theme of women's fantasies of possible escape from it, also appear in the early story 'The Child-Who-Was-Tired', published in 1910 and based closely on a tale by Chekhov, whom Katherine Mansfield regarded as her most important predecessor as a short-story writer. Again, there is an emphasis on fatigue as central to women's experience, and again fatigue acts as a catalyst for a utopian dream. But if Rosabel's utopia consisted of a stereotyped victory in an unchallenged vision of marriage as the way to material security and aesthetic satisfaction, the dream in this story is more troubled, more diffuse, while just as closely related to the conscious experience of the dreamer.

The story itself is simple, both in its portrayal of viciousness and in the direct response to it. The 'child' of the title is introduced in the first lines. She dreams of walking down 'a little road that led to nowhere' when a hand grabs her, and slaps and shakes her awake. The little girl pleads for sleep, but is tortured awake by her 'employer', a brutal woman who treats the child like a slave. The woman and her husband, while giving the child a life of threats and insults, pride themselves on their charity in taking her. The little girl is disgracefully 'free-born', illegitimate, and she has been 'rescued' from her natural mother who tried to kill her. The irony of this release into slavery is picked up in the ending of the story in which the child, driven by animal need for sleep, and half-pitying the incessant crying of the cruel couple's baby which is in her charge, smothers the infant, as she explains the desirability of death to it–"'You'll not cry any more nor wake up in the night.'"[6] The baby dead, the child falls immediately to the floor, back into the dream of the little road, having given the one gift her own mother tried to give her – the gift of oblivion. Throughout the story, the brutal couple take pains to represent the child as mad while driving her to an insanity which will bring them perfect poetic retribution through the murder of their own child.

The fairy-tale quality of the story allows Katherine Mansfield to stress the mirroring and doubling which signal the most important meanings of the tale. The child is a double of her natural mother, but succeeding rather than failing to rid herself of the unwanted baby which is the immediate source of her suffering. But the child is also the double of the crying infant, smothered by false parents. The cruel couple, wicked step-parents, are themselves murderers of the spirit of the girl. From one point of view, 'The Child-Who-Was-Tired' is a classic parable about oppression in its crudest forms, specifically about the oppression of women and children who live outside the protection of patriarchal law. Psychologically, the story drives toward the moment of psychic assertion when the tormented individual refuses or deforms the role assigned to her by others, yet bases her revolt on a revision of forms she already knows.

The question of the 'madness' of the girl's act of murder is, of course, an important one. Like Hardy's Little Father Time who kills his siblings in *Jude the Obscure*, the child as murderer here is a fictional enactment of a pessimistic view of the future for a society that defines those outside its structures as less than human. The death of the baby is a symbol of the death of the future. But one must note too that the child brings death to the baby as a kindly, precious gift. The action of the child who is already outside the law because of her illegitimate birth is, as well, a heroic gesture of defiance at the law that offers her nothing. None of this is understood by the girl who simply takes what she needs because, finally, she must have peace, which she is willing to share profoundly with her victim. Again the reader has access to meanings unavailable to the characters. It is not the child who is mad, but the culture which attempts to immobilise her beneath an iron mask whose weight she cannot bear. The 'road to nowhere' in her dream both images the truth of her vulnerable condition and is a figure of utopia, a place that is literally 'nowhere', in which everything is unlike the world she inhabits. The story is finally 'about' the results of oppression on the unconscious and its eruption into the world in the face of suppressed need.

'The Child-Who-Was-Tired' is simultaneously a cautionary tale, a gesture of protest, and an account of the function of the psyche. The fantastical elements – the nameless characters, the timeless setting, the extremity of the action – emphasise the generality of the paradigmatic relationships in the story. As in 'The Tiredness of Rosabel' the experience of the main female figure is that of life as ordeal, and once again the material and emotional conditions of that life are refracted through dreams that are ultimately, in some ways, self-destructive. The terrible irony in 'Rosabel' is that the girl's dream of escape actually validates the system that entraps her; the 'doubling' technique in 'The Child' invites a reading where the vengeance in the girl's act of murder must also be interpreted as suicide. Both stories are less concerned with overt action than with meanings generated in semi-conscious states. And for the characters these meanings are culturally-grounded confusions that promote hysteria and self-destruction.

If these two stories present the dream states of female characters that free the dreamers only into distorted repetitions of their own experience, another story of 1910, 'How Pearl Button Was Kidnapped', provides an alternative utopian, rather than dystopian, dream.

'Pearl Button' is almost pure allegory. Again, this is a commentary on a child's freedom revoked by adults. It specifically treats the forces that construct stereotyped roles for women and the difficulty of escape from those roles. Pearl Button is a conventional little girl, swinging alone on a gate outside her parents' house, 'the House of Boxes' – an obvious image of confinement – singing a 'small song', and watching the dust of the street blown by the 'little winds' of a 'sunshiny day'. The diminutive vocabulary and the cadences of the prose are those of the child's mind itself, and the world is seen as she sees it, once again claiming, fairy-tale licence for the tale.

> Two big women came walking down the street. One was dressed in red and the other was dressed in yellow and green. They had pink handkerchiefs over their heads, and both of them carried a big flax basket of ferns. They had no shoes and stockings on, and they came walking along, slowly, because they were so fat, and talking to each other and always smiling.[7]

These two rather unusual fairy godmothers are dark, frightened of the House of Boxes, but friendly to Pearl. Their gay clothing and freedom from restraint signalled by their unshod feet, contrast strongly with Pearl's tidy 'feminine' pinafore frill, and with the life of Pearl's mother, who, as Pearl tells them, is "'in the kitchin, ironing-because-its-Tuesday'". The girl accepts the women's invitation to join them, and anticipating some sort of constraining order among all adults, wonders what they have in their House of Boxes. But instead of being told their rules Pearl is cuddled and taken to a log house, undivided by walls, which is full of dark people, both men and women, who seem to be engaged in only pleasant things. Taken by them to the sea, Pearl is at first frightened by its immensity; but the people comfort her, strip her of most of her confining clothes, and lead her to the sand to join them in digging for shells, smiling all the time: "'Haven't you got any Houses of Boxes?" she said. "Don't you all live in a row? Don't the men go to offices? Aren't there any nasty things?'" It seems there are not. Nastiness reappears only with the arrival of the rescue-party from the world of Boxes. Pearl screams as 'Little men in blue coats – little men came running, running towards her with shouts and whistlings – a crowd of little blue men to carry her back to the House of Boxes.'[8] The police, emphatically male guardians of conventional regimentation, arrive to turn the idyll into nightmare.

The salient features of this story belong to the romantic tradition that glorifies the 'naturalness' and 'freedom' of the savage over the inhibitions and pleasure-denying aspects of mechanical civilisation. The story is clear in uniting the non-white and the as yet unsubdued girl-child as natural allies against the authority of patriarchy represented by the police. The world of the 'dark people', who are also the 'people' of the unconscious, is kind, vivid, open to pleasure, unregulated in the relations between the sexes. The dangerous blue of the police is contrasted with the magical blue of the sea which turns to crystal clarity in Pearl's cupped hands, a dream-like reflection of the beauty of the free unconscious when innocent of the strictures embodied by the orderly town.

Katherine Mansfield is using her 'dark people' for the same purpose as Dickens's circus people in *Hard Times*, and George Eliot's and D.H. Lawrence's gypsies. What is significant about all these 'wild' people is that they serve as foils to the conventional life that surrounds them. Representing liberty over enslavement, the unconscious over consciousness, free pleasure over artificially constructed pain, nature over civilisation, spontaneity over conformity, sexual response over rejection of sexuality, these untamed people stand as testaments to all the positive values that established society refuses. Pearl, who is not kidnapped at all, rather *escapes* from the world of masks into the world of freedom, only to be forced by the police, as if she was a criminal, to abandon her loosely structured utopia to be schooled into the rigid categories of women 'ironing-because-its-Tuesday' and men who inevitably 'go to offices'. The story should be bracketed with Mark Twain's *Huck Finn* and Henry James's *What Maisie Knew* as a treatment of the child as the image of humanity fettered rather than freed by culture. 'Pearl Button' is only a little over four pages long, but its poetic deftness, its original handling of traditional themes, and its firm sense of direction and alliance, make it important in Katherine Mansfield's development.

Two more stories about children from the early period deserve attention. 'New Dresses' (1911) and 'The Little Girl' (1912), are both only partially successful. But both anticipate, in interesting ways, the major stories that follow them. They are family stories and one of the most notable features of Katherine Mansfield's typical portrayal of family politics is that she adds to the usual configuration of mother, father and child, a fourth element in the figure of the grandmother. Katherine Mansfield's grandmothers are almost always widows and almost always residents in their daughters' houses. At times they are presented as matriarchs of profound strength, without whose presence the rest of the family could not function. At other times they are barely tolerated by the younger adults who treat them as superannuated fossils whose existence is best ignored. They are always crucial for the girl-child. And Katherine Mansfield shows them as loving beyond the powers of those who are still personally locked in the details of the sexual alternation of repulsion and desire.

Further, the grandmother is always a figure of justice in the stories, an impartial observer whose judgements, while often slighted, always run true. While remaining important to her adult daughter, the grandmother is usually of most significance to her granddaughter, who depends on the wisdom of the old woman to survive as an individual under the pressure placed upon her by her parents. There is often something almost penitent about the grandmother as she watches her usually frustrated daughter entrapped by marital subservience. It is almost as if, having sold her daughter into the slavery of convention, the old woman has decided to work differently for the child, while recognising too the forces of culture and temperament which will change her purposeful manoeuvres into something unforeseen. She offers a model of a different *kind* of relationship to those based on class or sexual power struggles. The grandmother is unselfish, a respecter of persons by necessity and through knowledge. She serves the same purpose for the reader as she does for the child – she is the single, dependable source of love in the stories, and a shrewd perceiver of hidden motives.

'New Dresses' is a broad feminist satire, in which Katherine Mansfield uses the doubling strategies already seen in 'The Child-Who-Was-Tired' to outline a psychological map of the modern family. The grandmother in the story shares her role with a kindly old man, Dr Malcolm, both of whom take the part of Helen, the little girl who is the scapegoat of the family. The issue at hand is that of new dresses for Helen and her sister, Rose. Anne, Helen's mother, has spent too much money on the cloth, and she nervously tries to displace her anxiety about her husband's reaction to her spending onto her child. Anne's favourite pastime is, in fact, complaining about Helen and her unladylike ways. Helen is grubby, Helen is disrespectful, Helen looks at her brother – known simply as 'Boy' – in a 'peculiar way'. Helen also stutters, and Anne means to take her to the doctor about it, '"if only to give her a good fright"'. Helen is perceived by Anne and her husband, Henry, as uncooperative in assuming the docility and passivity they expect from a girl.

45

The grandmother understands this, and implies an unstated link to her daughter after Anne makes the threat to frighten Helen with the male authority of the doctor. '"Anne,"' she says, '"you know she's always stuttered. You did just the same when you were her age, she's highly strung."'[9] Via the grandmother, Katherine Mansfield signals Anne's unwanted and unresolved identification with her rebellious daughter. For Anne, Helen is the self she has lost, the possible other if stammering self that has been submerged in her marriage to Henry, and which she now expresses only in furtive overspending and in constant denigration of rebellious traits in Helen. Anne's persecution of Helen is a devious persecution of abandoned parts of her own potentiality which she unconsciously craves to unloose, while her conscious self holds her in check by refusing to admit the real ignominy of her particular kind of marriage.

The humiliating nature of the marriage is revealed with the arrival of Henry, whom Katherine Mansfield presents in a series of masculine clichés as he returns beery and reeking of cigars after a jolly night out at the Political League. Henry, a caricatured patriarch, quickly seizes his opportunity to criticise his wife's talents as resident consumer in a crude speech in which Katherine Mansfield satirises the major features of sexist domination point by point:

'Good God! Anybody would think you'd married a millionaire. You could buy your mother a trousseau with that money. You're making yourself the laughing-stock for the whole town. How do you think I can buy Boy a chair or anything else – if you chuck away my earnings like that? Time and again you impress upon me the impossibility of keeping Helen decent; and then you go decking her out the next moment in thirty-five shillings' worth of green cashmere . . .'

On and on stormed the voice.[10]

This parody of patriarchal rage turns on a series of double binds as well as mutual blackmail. The source of Henry's power is money and he emphasises this in a way that calls the entire community to witness his rights. 'Boy' is identified as the only important child with maximum rights to his father's wealth. The sarcastic cut against the grandmother indirectly sneers at her probable lack of use for a trousseau and her dependent female status. Henry indulges in creating an undercurrent of threat as well as pleasuring in his righteous anger. But, most interestingly, Anne's attitude to Helen is thrown up as a reason for her to be contrite. If Anne will continue to condemn all that Helen stands for – and punish Helen accordingly – all might be well.

The satirical presentation of schooling into male and female roles continues. The next day Boy bangs tediously on his high chair while Henry proudly looks on. He encourages his son despite, or rather in defiance of, his wife's annoyance–"'Go it, old man. Tell mother boys like to kick up a row.'" Anne again displaces her feelings by warming to the sight of the girls – 'She could not help thrilling, they looked so very superior.' Anne settles for the soothing thought of class supremacy that goes along with acceptance of her subservience, and in a further displacement tells herself she's pleased because the girls look 'worthy' of their father. She silently tries to convey her submission to Henry: 'It was for your sake I made the dresses; of course you can't understand that, but *really* Henry.'[11]

Katherine Mansfield stresses the sadism in patriarchal 'love' as Henry goes to bully Helen in the girls' bedroom after she has torn her new dress in rough play

47

inconsistent with the role her parents have planned for her, and hidden the evidence of her 'crime'. Helen hears Henry

> come creaking into their room and hid under the bedclothes. But Rose betrayed her.
> 'Helen's not asleep,' piped Rose.
> Henry sat by the bedside, pulling his moustache.
> 'If it were not Sunday, Helen, I would whip you. As it is, and I must be at the office early to-morrow, I shall give you a sound smacking after tea in the evening . . . Do you hear me?'
> She grunted.
> 'You love your father and mother, don't you?'
> No answer.
> Rose gave Helen a dig with her foot.
> 'Well,' said Henry, sighing deeply, 'I suppose you love Jesus?'
> 'Rose has scratched my leg with her toe-nail,' answered Helen.
> Henry strode out of the room.[12]

Katherine Mansfield associates punishment, religious coercion, and conventional obedience to parents as facets of the same sick structure bent on extinguishing Helen's autonomy. At the same time she allows her reader a pleasurable snicker of sympathy with the child's resistance to that structure. Katherine Mansfield uses humour here as a weapon of revolt and release, a typical strategy in women's writing from Jane Austen to Margaret Atwood, and does so in ways that are very much part of a recognisable tradition of subversion of sexist hegemony.

'New Dresses' ends with the old people trying to make amends to Helen. Dr Malcolm arrives at the house with a copy of the torn dress while the grandmother tells him she is going to comfort Helen with a new doll to make up for her whipping. The old, conventionally 'wise' people distance themselves from the imposition of female docility and take their own subversive stands against the parents and in support of the girl's rebelliousness.

The interest in 'New Dresses', which is a qualified success despite its overly diagrammatic satire of the patriarchal family, is in Katherine Mansfield's ferocious comedy, her presentation of Anne's confused consciousness, and in the evocation of the sadistic edge in the schooling into gender.

By now it should be clear how closely Katherine Mansfield's early fiction is engaged in feminist issues and how various her experiments with strategies for writing about those issues were. Her repeated attention to the formation of female consciousness is especially sensitive and in a number of her early stories she confronts the question of how, given the cruelty of sexist relations between men and women, the roots of female desire for a male are ever established. That men are to be feared is clear from her treatment of patriarchy; that they might be loved is by no means self-evident.

Katherine Mansfield's attitude toward this subject is often related to her own love-hate relationship with her father, who, by all accounts, seems to have been the epitome of the Victorian bourgeois *paterfamilias* and simultaneously a man of some imagination and generosity. But given the analysis of the *general* state of relations between men and women in the fiction, Katherine Mansfield's interest does not demand an explanation so exclusively tied to her family background.

Some of the devices in 'New Dresses' surface again in 'The Little Girl', another early story about the education of a female child. The story marks the first appearance of a recurring figure in Katherine Mansfield's fiction–

Kezia, the girl-child in quest. Again, the family configuration of mother, father, grandmother and girl is drawn, and the story traces the psychological process of Kezia's shift from pure fear of her father to positive response to him via her imagining of aspects of commonality in their experience.

To Kezia, her father is 'to be feared and avoided', and she is relieved when he is out of the house. Again, the girl is portrayed as stuttering and liable to punishment for unintentional crimes. Kezia falls foul of her father while making his birthday present, a pin cushion which she unfortunately stuffs with shredded bits of his papers. She is, of course, punished. Whipped by her father she goes to her grandmother for comfort and explanation:

> 'What did Jesus make fathers for?' she sobbed.
> 'Here's a clean hanky, darling, with some of my lavender water on it. Go to sleep, pet; you'll forget all about it in the morning. I tried to explain to father, but he was too upset to listen tonight.'
> But the child never forgot. Next time she saw him she whipped both hands behind her back, and a red colour flew to her cheeks.[13]

Grandmother's policy of appeasement does not work; but what does is the father's offer of succour rather than hostility. In the absence of her mother and grandmother, Kezia has her repeated nightmare about 'the butcher with a knife and rope', a dream of terror about the male as devourer. Since the women are gone, Kezia accepts the comfort of her father who falls asleep beside her.

> Poor father! Not so big, after all – and with no one to look after him . . . . He was harder than the grandmother, but it

was a nice hardness . . . . And every day he had to work. . . .
She had torn up all his beautiful writing. . . . She stirred
suddenly, and sighed.
'What's the matter?' asked father. 'Another dream?'
'Oh,' said the little girl, 'my head's on your heart; I can
hear it going. What a big heart you've got, father dear.'[14]

The ending plays too hard on what is, finally, a fairly
sticky sentimentality, but what Katherine Mansfield is
trying to do here is interesting. This is a story of
generational and sexual *rapprochement* based on Kezia's
imagining of commonality with her father rather than
on recognition of his superiority or his power. She draws
close to him as she perceives him as like herself – suffering, isolated, pitiable and, intriguingly, yet unthreat-
eningly, different. The sexual element, while submerged, is important, and suggests an account of the
genesis of female desire quite different from the
Freudian or Jungian accounts which still dominate
discussion of the subject. Katherine Mansfield here is
tentatively positing a female sexuality whose basis is
reflective, based on similarity rather than difference.
Although sexual difference appears as one factor in the
account, it is not the main factor, and the 'hardness' of
the father elicits curiosity in the girl rather than either
respect on fear. What this story gives the reader is an
opening into a new account of the links between male
and female Katherine Mansfield was to return to in her
later fiction.

Except for 'The Child-Who-Was Tired' all the early
stories considered so far did not see book publication
until 1924. For her contemporaries, Katherine Mansfield
was pre-eminently the author of her short-story
collection of 1911, *In a German Pension*. This volume

became something of a *bête noire* for Katherine Mansfield, locking her into a reputation for thematic and stylistic practices which she felt she outgrew. The *Pension* stories, without exception, treat the poverty, absurdity and bitterness of conventional male/female relations and do so with an aggressive satire that is less obvious in Katherine Mansfield's later work. In 1920 she disowned the collection, writing to Murray who wanted to have it reprinted that:

> I cannot have the *German Pension* republished under any circumstances. It is far too *immature* and I don't even acknowledge it today . . . it's not good enough . . . It's positively juvenile, and besides, it's not what I mean, it's a lie.[15]

But she sarcastically gave in regarding reprinted ten days later:

> Very well, Isabel about the *Pension*. But I must write an introduction saying that it is early early work, or just that it was written between certain years, because you know, Betsy love, it's nothing to be proud of.[16]

Again in 1922 she warned her agent off the book saying that she had 'just begun to persuade the reviewers that I don't like ugliness for ugliness' sake', and that the collection was full of 'youthful extravagance of expression and youthful disgust'.[17]

C.A. Hankin believes that Katherine Mansfield's reasons for distancing herself from the volume were based on her private life. Hankin argues that a distaste for the 'physical subjects' that dominate the book was grounded on Katherine Mansfield's ambivalence about her bisexuality, while her desire to destroy 'the personality and the past she wanted buried'[18] led her to turn on the literary productions of her earlier years. One can, of course, only speculate about Katherine Mansfield's motives, but here it is more useful to turn to her literary development than to the details of her life. The sharp satire of the *Pension* volume differs greatly from the lyrical technique that had become Katherine Mansfield's characteristic method by the 1920s. Further, after World War I, the stories were open to simple nationalist readings that could identify the Germans alone as guilty of the abuses she savages. Far from abandoning the attitudes in the *Pension* stories to a past she had left behind, Katherine Mansfield had refined them. She was unfair to the collection. While it does not have the sinuousness, the half-tones and muted gestures of her later fiction, it succeeds on its own terms as biting caricature of brutality, mutual exploitation and moral blindness.

The Germans in the stories are rank and rowdy animals, unconscious of their idiotic parodies of civilised behaviour. '"There is nothing like cherries for producing free saliva after trombone playing," ' a gallant Herr Professor tells the young woman narrator in 'The Modern Soul' (1911). As he chews and spits out the stones he does not wonder at her refusal of his offer to share them: ' "It is your innate female delicacy. . . . Or perhaps you do not care to eat the worms. All cherries contain worms." '[19] The Professor, a good representative of the men in the volume, thinks himself irresistible. The women at the spa in which many of the stories are set, entice and pursue the men with equally clumsy gestures. The comedy is robust, inventive, absurdist: it is like watching beached walruses at play.

A few of the stories, however, are unremittingly sombre. 'Frau Brechenmacher Attends a Wedding' (1911), the best piece in the collection, is a dark continuation of the themes established in the comic *Pension* stories. Its success, comments Sylvia Berkman, derives from its 'emotional violence–a savage pity expressed in terms of a harshness that drives the narrator to underline every revolting detail.'[20] The story certainly exudes anger about the historical and cultural position of women and with the processes that deny them autonomy and press them to court their own enslavement, while their male partners debase themselves as part of the same process. The anger that informs the story, and is captured in its bluntness, is part of its excellence. Katherine Mansfield is one of the first writers in the twentieth century to address straightforwardly the anger of women at the injustice of their treatment, and express it in a prose that refuses to soften the accounts of the varieties of women's emotional response to their subjection.

'Frau Brechenmacher' begins with the familiar scene of an adult woman training her little girl for female servitude. The Frau and her daughter work frantically to prepare demanding Herr Brechnmacher's clothes for a wedding. When the man arrives he faults their work and his wife's appearance, and sends her into the dark passage to dress while he preens himself in front of the only mirror. The Frau gives the lamp and her shawl to her daughter, passing the standard of womanhood to the prematurely adult creature who has already been denied a childhood. The girl is left to guard the four smaller children who represent both her mother's fate and her own only possible future. The wedding is a farce. The bride, who has been 'wild', and who has brought along her illegitimate daughter as a last gesture of defiance, is dressed in white, 'giving her the appearance of an iced cake all ready to be cut and served in neat little pieces to the bridegroom', while the air of the *Festsaal* is appropriately fetid, filled with the 'familiar festive smell' of 'beer and perspiration'. When Herr Brechenmacher presents the communal gift it winds up to be a sexual insult – a silver coffee pot containing 'a baby's bottle and two little cradles holding china dolls'. The matrons watch the proceedings from the sides of the hall like cattle, quietly bemoaning but never challenging their lot, '"Girls,"' says meek Frau Brechen-macher, '"have a lot to learn."'[21] She has learned her own lesson only too well; home again with her drunken husband, he reminds her of their wedding night.

> Herr Brechenmacher yawned and stretched himself, and then looked up at her, grinning.
> 'Remember the night we came home? You were an innocent one, you were.'
> 'Get along! Such a time ago I forget.' Well she remembered.
> 'Such a clout on the ear as you gave me . . . But I soon taught you.'
> 'Oh, don't start talking. You've too much beer. Come to bed.'
> He tilted back his chair, chuckling with laughter.
> 'That's not what you said to me that night. God, the trouble you gave me!'

The Frau goes to bed after looking at the children.

> 'Always the same,' she said – 'all over the world the same; but, God in heaven – but *stupid*.'
> Then even the memory of the wedding faded quite. She lay down on the bed and put her arm across her face like a child who expected to be hurt as Herr Brechenmacher lurched in.[22]

The story is close to the drama in the vividness of its

apprehension of the characters, and the recurrent theme is that of men hurting and maiming women. Marriage is equivalent to ritual slaughter here and the triple sacrifice of the matron, the bride and the little girl presents a barbaric picture of the life-cycle of women. Especially cruel is the heavy sense of imprisonment of the matrons which is only lifted to allow them to witness the humiliation of yet another woman at the wedding. The women are perceived purely as objects by their men – as servants, providers of rough pleasure and as breeding machines. Frau Brechenmacher's mask is heavy, and beneath it she is a tangle of inadmissible fears. She must hide her terror that others are laughing at her, her sense of weakness, her terror of her husband, and she is so caught in her own horrors that she cannot even think of communicating with the other women. All the wives are masks speaking to masks, dumb in their captivity under bestial sexual norms. The tale ends as it began, with the expected violation of a child, the torturing of Frau Brechenmacher's unconscious. The Frau asserts her humanity only through her fear, her stoicism and her silence.

The story, like many of Katherine Mansfield's, is shaped by contradictory pressures. The narrative itself, with its sympathetic, revelatory, outraged view of Frau Brechenmacher's trouble, exists on a completely different ideological plane from that of the world it describes. The method is related to irony but goes beyond it to suggest a fracturing in the realm of values that is signalled by the distance of the ethical commitment of the narration from the world it realistically describes. The story reveals its rage, as Berkman says, in its selection of detail, its unglossed accusations that derive from the brutality of the symbolic objects and actions described. Meaning is made through an indirect-ness that permeates the entirety of the narrative. Frau Brechenmacher's reactions to her situation – fear, submission, docility – while offered as typical, are rejected by the anger of the prose that reveals them. It is the *manner* of writing that posits an alternative response to the familiar situation of the woman in the story. Katherine Mansfield is testing a kind of writing that is suited to suggesting complex responses to the reader while the narrative surface remains simple. It is obvious how useful this kind of narrative is in the hands of a woman writing out of a sense of the difference of women's potential from her traditional subjection and enforced simplicity. It neither denies the sordidness of women's history nor accepts it as the only paradigm for the future; it initiates a new register in women's satire.

Two stories in the *Pension* collection look closely at the intersection of psychology and biology in men and women's reactions to women's fertility. 'At Lehmann's' (*c.* 1911) studies the awakening of a young girl to the meaning of her sexuality, while 'A Birthday' (1911) portrays a man's response to his wife's labour. Both the stories contain protests against the idea of biologically determined destinies for women; both refuse to see women only as agents of reproduction.

Sabina, the jolly young waitress in 'At Lehmann's', is happy in her exploitative job and completely ignorant of her sexuality. The narrative is filtered through her consciousness as she good-naturedly does the cook's work as well as her own, wonders about gargantuan Frau Lehmann's pregnancy, and feels stirrings of incomprehensible reponse to a potential seducer who frequents the café. The seducer is impersonalised in the narrative, as he is in Sabina's mind, and known simply as the 'Young Man'. Sabina's response to him is both impersonal and unconscious, signalled in the text by actions that become symbols as she lets herself be lured into the secret warmth of the ladies' cloakroom, and stokes the fire high. The Young Man is puzzled by her but moves in to take his advantage:

> 'Look here,' he said roughly, 'are you a child, or are you playing at being one?'
> 'I–I–'
> Laughter ceased. She looked up at him once, then down at the floor, and began breathing like a frightened little animal.
> He pulled her closer still and kissed her mouth.
> 'Na, what are you doing?' she whispered.
> He let go her hands, he placed his on her breasts, and the room seemed to swim round Sabina. Suddenly, from the room above, a frightful, tearing shriek.
> She wrenched herself away, tightening herself, drew herself up.
> 'Who did that – who made that noise?'
> . . . . . .
> In the silence the thin wailing of a baby.
> 'Achk!' shrieked Sabina, rushing from the room.[23]

This ending of the story demands a symbolist reading as the association between lovemaking, the screams of the woman in childbirth, and the baby that wails its way into the world coalesce in the narrative to warn Sabina, without her conscious understanding, of her danger. Just precisely what Sabina 'knows' at the end of 'At Lehmann's' is uncertain; what the reader knows is that Katherine Mansfield has joined together images of male assault, female desire, pain, bewilderment and violence as the important aspects of a typical sexual initiation for women.

'A Birthday' traces a man's reaction to childbirth and fatherhood. The story follows the mind of Andreas

Bitzer as his wife suffers through the last stages of labour. The narrative concentrates on the husband's egoism and self-regard, and mocks his self-pity and annoyance with his wife's thoughtlessly interrupting his comfortable existence by giving birth to his third child. As in 'New Dresses' a corrective voice is given to an old doctor as Andreas whines about his wife's 'weakness'.

> 'Pity – this weather', said Doctor Erb.
> 'Yes, it gets on Anna's nerves, and it's just nerve she wants.'
> 'Eh, what's that?' retorted the doctor. 'Nerve! Man alive! She's got twice the nerve of you and me rolled into one. Nerve! she's nothing but nerve. A woman who works as she does about the house and has three children in four years thrown in with the dusting, so to speak. . . !'
> 'Now *he's* accusing me,' thought Andreas. 'That's the second time this morning – first mother and now this man taking advantage of my sensitiveness.[24]

Andreas's ill-expressed and ill-channelled but real feelings of helplessness are only partly concealed by his mental bluster. His insensitivity, which he mistakes for delicacy, announces his own vulnerability. Under the cover of complaints Andreas tries to admit to himself neither his feelings of dependence on his wife nor his knowledge that he has used her too hard. When the wife, after much pain, gives birth to the son he desires, Andreas seemingly irrelevantly says, '"Well, by God! Nobody can accuse *me* of not knowing what suffering is." '[25] Katherine Mansfield makes this bundle of constructs that represents a typical husband ridiculous, a parody of masculine selfishness and vanity. But there is also a shred of pity in the story for a character who needs so desperately to be validated by the constant presence of an enslaved wife, whose conformity to a particular male stereotype makes him a silly and vulnerable fool, and who yet shares in the paralysing terror of isolation that she sees as the most central feature of the human condition.

If Katherine Mansfield demonstrates a pervasive interest in recording the experience of women in her early work as well as an interest in discovering new ways to speak of that experience, the *Pension* stories also make it clear that she had no use for self-declared 'progressive' theories about women which claim that the signs of women's oppression are actually innate feminine virtues. In terms of locating herself in relation to the feminist movement of her time, 'An Advanced Lady' (*c.* 1911) is one of her most important stories. In this tale Katherine Mansfield parodies the platitudes of a traitorous 'feminism', pernicious in that its claims promote further entrapment of women. In the story the Advanced Lady herself goes for a walk with other residents in her hotel including the sceptical narrator. The Lady has left her daughter behind to sit alone in her room while she herself holds forth to the other guests about the book she is writing:

> 'The trouble is to know where to stop. My brain has been a hive for years, and about three months ago the pent-up waters burst over my soul, and since then I am writing all day until late into the night, still ever finding fresh inspirations and thoughts which beat impatient wings about my heart.'
> 'Is it a novel?' asked Else shyly.
> 'Of course it is a novel,' said I.
> 'How can you be so positive?' said Frau Kellermann, eyeing me severely.
> 'Because nothing but a novel could produce an effect like that.'

'Ach, don't quarrel,' said the Advanced Lady sweetly. 'Yes it is a novel–upon the Modern Woman. For this seems to me the woman's hour. It is mysterious and almost prophetic, it is the symbol of true advanced women; not one of those violent creatures who deny their sex and smother their frail wings under . . . under–'

'The English tailor-made?' from Frau Kellermann.

'I was not going to put it like that. Rather, under the lying garb of false masculinity!'

'Such a subtle distinction!' I murmured.

'What then,' asked Fräulein Elsa, looking adoringly at the Advanced Lady – 'whom then do you consider the true woman?'

'She is the incarnation of comprehending Love!'[26]

' "That theory of yours about women and Love," ' says the disgusted narrator near the end of the story," ' – it's as old as the hills – oh, older!" ' "I too," ' she says, ' "would like to write a book on the advisability of caring for daughters and taking them for airings and keeping them out of kitchens!" '[27] In effect, this is precisely what Katherine Mansfield herself is doing in the *Pension* stories.

The ideology in Katherine Mansfield's early writing is decidedly and overtly feminist and I can only comment that it is peculiar that this observation is not already a commonplace of Katherine Mansfield criticism. If, as Virginia Woolf suggests in *A Room of One's Own*, one of the tasks of the committed woman writer is to begin to transcribe 'the accumulation of unrecorded life'[28] that comprises most of women's lost history, then Katherine Mansfield surely saw herself from the beginning as one of those who broke that silence.

Although the concerns of Katherine Mansfield's early stories – whether fabular, satirical or realist – foreground women's experience, it is important, too, to note that they are not *limited* to it. No one could claim that issues of injustice, isolation, sexual unease or cruelty were the particular property of one sex, race or class. What is important is that Katherine Mansfield uses ordinary women's experiences as the starting-points from which to survey the world in general, and does so with a confidence that was to remain constant in her writing.

Chapter Three

'Prelude'

Katherine Mansfield wrote almost nothing between
1912 and 1915. When she seriously began publishing
again in 1917 her writing had been transformed. Her
writer's block, which seems to have stemmed from a
complex tangle of miseries – illness, financial instability,
disillusionment with friends, the nightmare of the war,
uncertainty about her commitment to Murry, constant
moving – broke in 1915 when she was in Paris a month
after the end of a short-lived love affair. The story that
was begun in 1915 as 'The Aloe' and finally published by
Virginia and Leonard Woolf's Hogarth Press in 1918 as
'Prelude' was a breakthrough for both Katherine
Mansfield and the short story in English. As Murry
notes, it was a story of 'revolutionary novelty'[1] whose
method diverged sharply from the traditional short-
story form, and which extended the techniques that
Katherine Mansfield had been using in her early stories.
   Katherine Mansfield herself was excited by the
composition of the story from the first. At the beginning

she conceived of it as the opening part of a novel, and its origin can be precisely dated from a letter to Murry of 25 March 1915:

> I had a great day yesterday. The Muses descended in a ring, like the angels on the Botticelli Nativity roof ... and I fell into the open arms of my first novel. I have finished a large chunk ... tell me what you think, won't you? It's queer stuff.... Yesterday I had a fair wallow in it, and then I shut my shop and went for a long walk along the Quai – very far. It was dusk when I started, but dark when I got home. The lights came out as I walked, and the boats danced by. Leaning over the bridge I suddenly discovered that one of those boats was exactly what I want my novel to be. Not big, almost 'grotesque' in shape – I mean perhaps heavy – with people rather dark and seen strangely as they move in the sharp light and shadow; and I want bright shivering lights in it, and the sound of water.[2]

The finished story is faithful to what Katherine Mansfield describes here in a vocabulary of images. An impressionistic impulse is behind 'Prelude'; the characters are presented in terms of the intersection of light and shade, and seen fleetingly against the light of the stars and the evanescent mystery of the sea. Identity in the story is as impermanent as the dappled moments in a Renoir or a Manet, and the temporary look of things – people, objects, social relations – is all that the narrative claims to know with any certainty. In 'Prelude' Katherine Mansfield emphasises the lack of fixture in life–the vagaries of perception, the way that consciousness is invaded in surprising ways by unconscious forces, the almost limitless possibilities for change, the poverty of static assumptions. These things are the centre of gravity for the story, and how little her own conception of the writing changed between 1915 and the completion of 'Prelude' in 1917 can be seen from the letter she wrote to Dorothy Brett when the manuscript had been delivered to the Woolfs.

'What form is it?' you ask. Ah, Brett, it's so difficult to say. As far as I know, it's more or less my own invention. And 'How have I shaped it?' This is about as much as I can say about it. You know, if the truth were known I have a perfect passion for the island where I was born. Well, in the early morning there I always remember feeling that this little island has dipped back into the dark blue sea during the night only to rise again at gleam of day, all hung with bright spangles and glittering drops . . . . I tried to catch that moment–with something of its sparkle and its flavour. And just as on those mornings white milky mists rise and uncover some beauty, then smother it again and then again disclose it, I tried to lift that mist from my people and let them be seen and then to hide them again . . . It's so difficult to describe all this and it sounds perhaps overambitious and vain. But I don't feel anything but intensely a longing to serve my subject as well as I can.[3]

Again Katherine Mansfield describes the story in visual, impressionistic terms, and this description is useful in understanding what she was trying to do.

What is so impressive about Katherine Mansfield's writing in 'Prelude' is that she succeeded in devising a kind of narration that exactly mirrors the consciousnesses of her characters, and which keeps this connection unbroken even in passages of description. That she saw the need for such a technique is evident as early as 'The Tiredness of Rosabel', but it is only in 'Prelude' that she demonstrates her mature capacity to make it work without deviation. Images and symbols, as well as rational thoughts, are tied to particular characters, and this allows Katherine Mansfield to suggest the movements of the characters' *unconscious* states to the reader without recourse to discursive explanation. This extension of the indirect free style (which had been a common practice in fiction throughout the nineteenth century even though it is often mistakenly labelled as a twentieth-century device) is itself a statement about the nature of experience, which is not only *declared* to be an amalgamation of conscious and unconscious modes, but is *written* as such. The technique allows language to embody non-verbal experience; it pushes prose into an area usually accessible only to poetry.

This is undoubtedly what Katherine Mansfield meant in an often-quoted journal entry written while she was working on 'Prelude'. The entry is usually cited as evidence of her desire to make the story a memorial for her dead brother, and to create an image of New Zealand – an 'undiscovered country' – which could not be dismissed in Europe. And certainly, these intentions are stated in the highly nostalgic entry which is partially written as a message to the lost brother. But what seems more interesting is her linking of her work on 'Prelude' with something she saw as a poetic impulse.

> Then I want to write poetry. I feel always trembling on the brink of poetry. The almond tree, the birds, the little wood where you are, the flowers you do not see . . . . But especially I want to write a kind of long elegy to you . . . perhaps not in poetry. Nor perhaps in prose. Almost certainly in a kind of *special* prose.[4]

These images do find their way into 'Prelude', but for quite different reasons than one might expect, given Katherine Mansfield's accounts of the process of writing the story.

The dreaminess in her letters and journal entries concerning 'Prelude' reflect its beauty but make few helpful comments on the dangerous meanings of the story. As a reader of Katherine Mansfield might guess, this study of a family (based on Katherine Mansfield's own family) is a highly critical one, and the intricacies of technique, applied in the story to deceptively trivial matters, are used to present a picture of family politics that is radically subversive. As Willa Cather commented in a very perceptive reading of 'Prelude', the story is about the terrors, more than the pleasures, of family life:

> I doubt whether any contemporary writer has made one feel more keenly the many kinds of personal relations in an everyday 'happy family' who are merely going on living their daily lives, with no crises or shocks or bewildering complications to try them. Yet every individual in the household (even the children) is clinging passionately to his individual soul, is in terror of losing it in the general family flavour. As in most families, the mere struggle to have anything of one's own, to be one's self at all, creates an element of strain which keeps everybody almost at the breaking-point.[5]

'Prelude' is, in fact, a very odd sort of elegy. It is a story about freedom under threat, of the pull of 'group life' (set in stereotyped forms which the characters try to impose on each other and to escape from themselves) as against the life of the autonomous individual. And again, as in the early stories, Katherine Mansfield's focus is on the women and girls – their bonds, their struggles to find their identities, the masks they wear and the ways they perceive the world.

'Prelude' begins on the Burnells' moving day. Moving house is itself used as a metaphor for the possibility of change as the characters are temporarily dislodged from their habits and set roles. As is often the case in reading women's writing, the domesticity of the scene has been taken as a sign of nostalgic triviality and sentimentality rather than for what it most certainly suggests – an occasion of defamiliarisation and estrangement from previous selves and circumstances that prompts a series of moments of self-awareness for the characters. Three generations of women are at the heart of the story. Mrs Fairchild is the apotheosis of all of Katherine Mansfield's grandmothers – matriarchal, witch-like, eminently competent and loving. Linda is woman-as-wife, the woman of childbearing age, lost in a nightmare of fertility, the passionately desired prey of her robustly animal husband. Linda's sister, Beryl, is unmarried and desperate for the social definition of a husband and house of her own, and desperate too for romance and sexual experience. The little girls, Linda's children, are more fluid, though they contain the seeds of a range of typical possibilities for women. Isabel likes to be ladylike and 'grown up'; Lottie is a pathetic bundle of timidity who invites bullying; and Kezia is the Wordsworthian child (after all, the story is named 'Prelude'), who wonders at the world and who is alternately shocked and delighted by her explorations.[6]

The network of images in 'Prelude', which draws on both conventional and original usages, is brilliantly controlled and allows Katherine Mansfield to invest ordinary objects with great, suggestive complexity as functions of the minds of her characters. Bright, floating stars, a dancing sea and incomprehensible voices in the night, are used to suggest yet another order of experience to which none of the characters has access. The moon, talismanic of the grandmother, presides over the scene, and in the garden, barbed and mysterious, the great aloe, associated primarily with Linda and Kezia, dominates the narrative.

Each of the eleven sections of 'Prelude' concerns itself with a small slice of the Burnells' life. Like Katherine Mansfield's early work dealing with children, many of the sections are about education into dominance and submission in terms of class, sex and age, and are punctuated with moments that deny the permanence of such divisions. The children are amusing without being sentimentalised (this was a constant danger for Katherine Mansfield, who shared the general modernist distrust of sentiment; as she complained in a letter in 1921 'the kind of sentimental writing about virginia creeper and the small haigh voices of tainy children is more than I can stick').[7] The children, especially together, are in fact brutal parodies of the adults. The exception is Kezia, the most important single figure in the story, and the adults all function as teachers and potential teachers for the child's still open mind.

The first section opens, significantly, with Kezia being left behind with her sister Lottie by her mother and grandmother who cannot find space in the buggy to take them to the new house. Left amid the chaos of 'the tables and chairs standing on their heads on the front lawn',[8] the first of a series of images of disruption, they are taken in hand by an asthmatic neighbour who gives them tea with her boys. Kezia dislikes the neighbour and her sons for reasons that are obvious as soon as she sits down in the nursery:

> Moses grinned and gave her a nip as she sat down; but she pretended not to notice. She did hate boys.
> 'Which will you have?' asked Stanley, leaning across the table very politely, and smiling at her. 'Which will you have to begin with – strawberries and cream or bread and dripping?'
> 'Strawberries and cream, please,' said she.
> 'Ah-h-h-h.' How they all laughed and beat the table with their teaspoons. Wasn't that a take-in! Wasn't it now! Didn't he fox her! Good old Stan!
> 'Ma! She thought it was real.'

Even Mrs.Samuel Josephs, pouring out the milk and water could not help smiling. 'You busn't tease theb on their last day,' she wheezed[9]

This scene sends reverberations through the story; it reflects what Brigid Brophy has called Katherine Mansfield's 'cannibal imagination'[10] – her persistent association of eating with cruelty. Rather than show her feelings, Kezia devours her own tear in a gesture of emotional self-consumption that also sends ripples of meaning through the story. The little boy, Stanley, is indulged in his petty bullying by his mother just as the adult Stanley Burnell, Kezia's father, is indulged in his corresponding appetitiveness by the women who are likewise humiliated by him. Stanley Burnell is closely associated with devouring things too–the cherries that he pretends to share with his wife but gobbles himself; the pork chops he smacks down while Linda is unable to eat; the duck, sign of mortality and human destruction for Kezia, that he carves with artistic sadism. In delineating this calm, everyday world, Katherine Mansfield, like Sylvia Plath, pairs destruction and desire as the most normal of associations. Both of the Stanleys offer sustenance to women that they not only fail to deliver, but offer falsely in the first place. Kezia, not yet bowed, eats her own tear as her mother consumes herself in response to the appetite of her husband.

Night arrives and the girls are driven to the new house by a kindly storeman. Kezia questions him closely: '"Do the stars ever blow about?"' she asks. '"Not to notice,"' he replies.[11] The contrast between the fixity of the stars, or at least the human incapacity to comprehend their movements, initiates another theme, that of the characters' attempts to impose an order on the world that will be in some kind of harmony with the natural world. But, unlike the dark people in 'Pearl Button', whose ideas of order fit the natural images around them, the Burnells' rural utopia will be structured by the cultural patterns they have already internalised. The 'strangeness' represented by the move is denied by the human consciousnesses which resist being unsettled internally if not externally. But if, for most of the characters, the new house is already the recognisable territory of a patriarchal, bourgeois, colonial family before the boxes are even unloaded, it suggests other possibilities to Kezia. To her it is a magic place, the unknown, a wonderland where her unconscious will confront a world yet untamed by definition.

Kezia first sees the house as a vague outline with flickering shapes moving in it. Mrs Fairfield meets the children at the door and hands Kezia one of the lamps, transmitting her 'light' to her grandchild in one of the many gestures that identifies Kezia as the heiress to her grandmother's knowledge. The other members of the family come into focus as Kezia adjusts to the dim light: Linda suffers with a headache; Aunt Beryl demands that Kezia relinquish the lamp (just as Beryl throughout the story tries to compensate for her own half-understood misery by snatching happiness from others); Stanley calls for more food, gloats over his pork chops, and narcissistically admires his own powers of digestion. The whole family retires: Lottie and Isabel argue about whether God will accept prayers said in bed; Kezia tells her grandmother to '"Come to bed soon and be my Indian brave"'; Beryl dreams of a young man in the garden who has come for her; Linda and Stanley both perform the ritual of admiring Stanley's business acumen. The last to bed is the grandmother, who sighs and takes out her teeth as she joins Kezia, while sounds in the garden close this initial section of the story.

In the garden some tiny owls, perched on the branches of
a lace-bark tree, called: 'More pork; more pork.' And far
away in the bush there sounded a harsh rapid chatter: 'Ha-
ha-ha . . . Ha-ha-ha.'[12]

The voices of nature perfectly mimic the unconscious
situation of the Burnells. The varieties of conventional
and unconventional sexual ritual performed by the
entire group before they sleep is subsumed in the
antipodean '"more pork"' of the wise little owls, echoing
Stanley's feats of digestion earlier in the evening, and
the general impulse to devour one another prevalent in
the family as a whole. The sardonic laugh that ends the
section is as much the comment of the author as that of
nature itself on the Burnells' arrangements, and perhaps
those of humanity in general. The grandmother, the
only character who understands the situation with any
clarity, has no teeth, and the night laughs at her as much
as it does the less comprehending members of the finally
sleeping family.

'Prelude' is filled with images of birds. Linda dreams of
a baby bird that becomes a monstrous child, Mrs
Fairfield wears a necklace with a crescent moon and five
little owls suggesting her witch-like powers of imposing
order on the world, the trees are full of birds, the
wallpaper's pattern is of flying parrots, Beryl sings a
song about birds. Wings beat through the pages of
'Prelude'. They signal desire for flight and freedom, and
prepare the reader for one of the two central incidents in
the story. The little girls and their two male cousins are
invited by the hired man, Pat, to see '"how the kings of
Ireland chop the head off a duck"'. The children straggle
along, curious if cautious, to what will be an initiation
into the savagery of everyday life.

There was an old stump beside the door of the fowl-house. Pat grabbed the duck by the legs, laid it flat across the stump, and almost at the same moment down came the little tomahawk and the duck's head flew off the stump. Up the blood spurted over the white feathers and over his hand.

When the children saw the blood they were frightened no longer. They crowded round him and began to scream. Even Isabel leaped about crying: 'The blood! The blood!' Pip forgot all about his duck. He simply threw it away from him and shouted, 'I saw it. I saw it,' and jumped round the wood block.

Rags, with cheeks as white as paper, ran up to the little head, put out a finger as if he wanted to touch it, shrank back again and then again put out a finger. He was shivering all over.

Even Lottie, frightened little Lottie, began to laugh and pointed at the duck and shrieked: 'Look, Kezia, look.'

'Watch it!' shouted Pat. He put down the body and it began to waddle–with only a long spurt of blood where the head had been; it began to pad away without a sound towards the steep bank that led to the stream . . . . That was the crowning wonder.

'Do you see that? Do you see that?' yelled Pip. He ran among the little girls tugging at their pinafores.

'It's like a little engine. It's like a funny little railway engine,' squealed Isabel.

But Kezia suddenly rushed at Pat and flung her arms around his legs and buried her head as hard as she could against his knees.

'Put head back! Put head back!' she screamed.

When he stooped to move her she would not let go or take her head away. She held on as hard as she could and sobbed: 'Head back! Head back!' until it sounded like a loud strange hiccup.[13]

The children react uneasily to Kezia's outburst as they

simmer down from their blood-lust and return to their 'civilised' personalities. They scatter, ashamed at their own responses. Kezia is finally comforted by Pat after noticing his 'little round gold ear-rings. She never knew that men wore ear-rings.She was very much surprised.'[14]

The scene is a *tour de force*. Most obviously, it is a fine piece of psychological realism, with Pat, who genuinely likes children, and who only thinks to entertain them, finding himself the catalyst for igniting their most barbaric responses. Pat is the representative of all the adults, blind to the possibilities of meaning in his action, defining himself as wholly benign, unaware of the unconscious satisfactions in the killing that the not fully acculturated children openly express. The children's excitement at their inclusion in an adult 'rite' of death is important too; they recognise power when they see it and respond with horrible glee. This is not the conventionally imagined world of the Victorian child despite 'Prelude's' nineteenth-century setting: it is the child's world as imagined in this century in Golding's *Lord of the Flies*, Christina Stead's *The Man Who Loved Children* or Richard Hughes' *High Wind in Jamaica* in which children are formulations for a ferocious view of the human unconscious. But Kezia, and *her* reaction, is convincing as a possible alternative response. In this very ritualistic scene she assumes the position of suppliant before the man who has demonstrated his power of imposing death in an ordinary yet godlike display of authority. The scene is of a primal fall from innocence, and it is also a scene in which a male parent-figure initiates the children into slaughter. In 'Prelude' this is the core of masculine gender. The male is the devourer of life, the killer, and Pat's act is completed as male ritual later in the story when we see Stanley – associated with knives like the butcher in Kezia's nightmare in 'The Little Girl' – carving the same duck with professional manly pleasure.

Kezia is only recalled from her terror through the evidence of Pat's likeness to women. Katherine Mansfield here is making the same point as she did in 'The Little Girl'. Kezia does not revise her response to the killing of the duck; she shifts her attention away from it to Pat's ear-rings. The male as killer remains incomprehensible; the man with the ear-rings is not. She fixes on this seemingly discontinuous element of commonality and it draws her back from her hysteria in the face of what she has just learned. We are dealing in this episode – as in the scene in Proust's *Remembrance of Things Past* where the servant Françoise literally murders a chicken – not only with the unconscious reaction to death, but with its relationship to the author's understanding of the mechanism of sexual order in her culture.

The single most important image in 'Prelude' is the aloe and the first scene concerning it is vital. It dramatises Kezia's only moment of significant contact with her mother. Kezia in 'Prelude', as in most of the Burnell stories, is usually in closer external contact with her grandmother, but she shares with her mother an imaginative intensity that is the most absorbing part of life for both characters. As Kezia wanders in the garden and explores the patterns of its beds, finding the place where the tamed gives way to the untamed, she comes upon a mysterious plant as her mother floats up the path toward her.

'Mother, what is it?' asked Kezia.
Linda looked up at the fat swelling plant with its cruel leaves and fleshy stem. High above them, as though becalmed in the air, and yet holding so fast to the earth it grew from, it might have had claws instead of roots. The

curving leaves seemed to be hiding something; the blind stem cut into the air as if no wind could ever shake it.

'That is an aloe, Kezia,' said her mother.

'Does it ever have any flowers?'

'Yes, Kezia,' and Linda smiled down at her, and half shut her eyes. 'Once every hundred years.'[15]

These are the only words exchanged by the mother and daughter in the story, their only moment of real connection. As Kezia wonders at the plant and asks her mother for interpretative guidance, Linda can give almost nothing – only a few words and a languid smile, as she gives the aloe her own meaning – one of female strength. Kezia cannot know this, and her mother has no way to communicate her inchoate private meaning even if she wished. The result is a mystery, not only the mystery inherent in nature, but also mystification between mother and daughter that denies direct verbal communication and the building of a female tradition of interpreting the world. But there is another kind of communication going on all the same; Kezia *can* see her mother's smile in response to the cruel plant. The connection she must make, if she makes it at all, must be wordless, unspoken, but no less valuable for that.

It must be stressed again how important Kezia is as a recurring figure in Katherine Mansfield's writing. She is the girl-child who is in the process of being deformed into one of the wounded and wounding adults who populate the fiction; but she is also a figure who resists that deformation and who retains the capacity for other sorts of human possibilities. She is also a strong figure of the unconscious, with pure needs, pure desires that run counter to the processes of her education and which are not extinguished despite multiple conflicts and confusions.

'Prelude'

Linda, on the other hand, is an older, baffled Kezia, a cornered Kezia, who lives in fear behind the hopelessly ill-fitting mask of a middle-class wife that reveals almost nothing of her true reactions to her experience. Linda Burnell in 'Prelude' is one of the finest examples Katherine Mansfield ever drew of the disintegration caused by sexuality perceived as bondage, and the character is almost a complete expression of the author's mature views on the subject, made possible by the evolution of her style. Linda is radically confused by the contradictions between her fractured responses to life and the conventional code of wife and mother that is supposed to inform her existence. Her husband, Stanley, as has been seen, is largely presented as an affectionate male ogre, selfishly devouring everything in his path. He is supported and suspended in his stereotyped masculinity by Linda's being what she is – incapable, withdrawn into her imaginary life, hiding behind an exaggerated, enervated feminine passivity as extreme as Stanley's over-developed masculinity. Together, they sustain each other in their ordinary monstrousness. While Stanley is largely oblivious to his grotesqueness (and his consciousness is portrayed as correspondingly uncomplicated), Linda is constantly aware of her imprisonment within a life that she partly wants and partly rejects. Katherine Mansfield pays close attention to this psychological division that so torments Linda that it swallows up her consciousness, leaving room for little but contemplation of her miserable confusion.

The children are the visible sign of her trouble. In the first page of the story there is a note of giddiness in Linda's reaction to leaving the girls behind with the furniture:

the grandmother's lap was full and Linda Burnell could not

possibly have held a lump of a child on hers for any distance
. . .

'We shall simply have to leave them. That is all. We shall simply have to cast them off,' said Linda Burnell. A strange little laugh flew from her lips; she leaned back against the buttoned cushions and shut her eyes, her lips trembling with laughter.[16]

Linda's mixture of affection and distaste for her children is attended by an unease that constantly threatens to lapse into madness and usually exhibits itself as physical illness. When Kezia and Lottie arrive at the new house they are warned by their grandmother to be quiet: '"Poor little mother has got such a headache."' Linda, stretched out immobile in front of the fire, asks after the children but does 'not really care', does 'not even open her eyes to see.' Later, in bed with her husband, when she is embraced, 'her faint far-away voices seemed to come from a deep well.' The next day she consciously wishes she were going away, 'driving away from them all in a little buggy, driving away from everybody and not even waving'.[17]

Stanley seems to perceive his wife's languor and sickly delicacy as a form of sensuality. It is, in fact, the involuntary reaction of a woman living in terror of her body and its astounding, unwilled capacity to generate life. Her fertility undermines Linda's sense of who or what she is, and fills her with a dread that cannot be overcome because she cannot perceive its origin as a coherent function of herself. Her body is her enemy, collaborating with and subjected to the men, who, in her imagination as in her life, trigger its involuntary response. Linda is alienated, exposed, threatened, and she cannot see beyond the threat to any positive action. Her dream of the bird indicates the nature of her distress:

'How loud the birds are,' said Linda in her dream. She was walking with her father through a green paddock sprinkled with daisies. Suddenly he bent down and parted the grasses and showed her a tiny ball of fluff just at her feet. 'Oh, papa, the darling.' She made a cup of her hands and caught the tiny bird and stroked its head with her finger. It was quite tame. But a funny thing happened. As she stroked it began to swell, it ruffled and pouched, it grew bigger and bigger and its round eyes smiled knowingly at her. Now her arms were hardly wide enough to hold it and she dropped it into her apron. It had become a baby with a big naked head and a gaping bird-mouth, opening and shutting. Her father broke into a loud clattering laugh and she woke to see Burnell rattling the Venetian blind up to the very top.

'Hullo,' he said. 'Didn't wake you, did I?'[18]

Linda's dream is very much one of awakening, a forced awakening into biological fertility for which she is not ready, and which she neither understands nor desires. Under such circumstances it is no surprise that both her father, and, less consciously, her husband are imagined by her as monsters, savouring her discomfort, driving her truly mad in their lack of recognition of her psychological state. The whole world seems to conspire against her; 'things' for Linda, have 'a habit of coming alive':

Sometimes, when she had fallen asleep in the daytime, she woke and could not lift a finger, could not even turn her eyes to the left or right because THEY were there; sometimes when she went out of a room and left it empty, she knew as she clicked the door to that THEY were filling it up ... THEY knew how frightened she was; THEY saw how she turned her head away as she passed the mirror . . .

Yes, everything had come alive down to the minutest, tiniest particle, and she did not feel her bed, she floated, held up in the air. Only she seemed to be listening with her wide open watchful eyes, waiting for someone to come who just did not come, watching for something to happen that just did not happen.[19]

Linda's paranoia (and it is right to give it a pathological name) stems directly from a particular female role undertaken in bad faith. She hates the light, refuses knowledge, preferring the darkness that paralyses her, able, in the terms of her dream, to accept the toy-like 'tiny ball of fluff' but not the demanding bird/child. Linda is a victim of the myth of motherhood. She abandons her real children as they appear; she sees them as accidents forced upon her from without, horrible tricks that have been played on a self that would like to revert to a 'fluffy' world. Yet she also knows this is not possible. She is caught by a culture that offers such nonsense to women as the whole of reality and then laughs at them for believing it. Linda is a victim of female infantilisation, paradoxically a mother who can only function sanely as a child.

Linda tries to avoid her knowledge in various ways. There is her rejection of the children, of food, of activity; it is as if she feels that if she can keep very quiet, live as little as possible, then the need to live at all will pass her by, and allow her to evade the terrible 'THEY' who mysteriously make things grow. But her most significant response to her entrapment in a life over which she feels she has no control is in hatred, and it is for this reason, as a symbol of her utter hatred, that she identifies herself with the aloe. Able to think about it only at night and in her mother's clarifying presence she says:

'I like that aloe. I like it more than anything here. And I am sure I shall remember it long after I've forgotten all the other things.

She put her hand on her mother's arm and they walked
down the steps . . . she could see the long sharp thorns that
edged the aloe leaves, and at the sight of them her heart
grew hard . . . She particularly liked the long sharp thorns . .
. Nobody would dare to come near the ship or follow after.

'Not even my Newfoundland dog,' she thought, 'that I'm
so fond of in the daytime.'

For she really was fond of him; she loved and admired and
respected him tremendously. Oh, better than anyone else
in the world. She knew him through and through. He was
the soul of truth and decency, and for all his practical
experience he was awfully simple, easily pleased and easily
hurt . . .

If only he wouldn't jump at her so, and bark so loudly and
watch her with such eager, loving eyes. He was too strong
for her; and she had always hated things that rush at her,
from a child. There were times when he was frightening.
When she just had not screamed at the top of her voice:
'You are killing me.' And those times she had longed to say
the most coarse, hateful things . . .

'You know I'm very delicate. You know as well as I do that
my heart is affected, and the doctor has told you I may die
any moment. I have had three great lumps of children
already . . .'

Yes, yes, it was true. Linda snatched her hand from her
mother's arm. For all her love and respect and admiration
she hated him. And how tender he always was after times
like those, how submissive, how thoughtful . . . It had never
been so plain to her as it was at this moment . . . She could
have done her feelings up in little packets and given them to
Stanley. She longer to hand him that last one, for a surprise.
She could see his eyes as he opened that . . . [20]

As the narration slips effortlessly from speech to mind,
and from conscious control to unwilled response, and
moves as well from one emotionally-charged image or
idea to another, Katherine Mansfield leads us again to
what (as in the episode dealing with Pat and the duck) is

the central danger point of the entire story: the coalescence of sexuality and death. The 'nursery' view of the world that associates Stanley with the dog (and Linda *is* genuinely fond of this aspect of him) is of the same order of thought as that which betrays Linda in her sub-conscious view of child-bearing in the fluffy bird. In the night, however, the part of the truth that Linda ordinarily cannot confront reveals itself: Stanley's double, a Mr Hyde to his daytime Dr Jekyll, a rapacious sexual devourer, more wolf than dog, attacks her. Linda's psychological response is to fight death with death, to identify herself with the barbed aloe that would keep death at bay by dealing death itself.

This crucial passage echoes an earlier one involving Kezia. On her journey to the new house Kezia asks the storeman:

> 'What is the difference between a ram and a sheep?'
> 'Well, a ram has horns and runs for you.'
> Kezia considered. 'I don't want to see it frightfully,' she said. 'I hate rushing animals like dogs and parrots. I often dream that animals are rushing at me – even camels – and while they are rushing their heads swell e-enormous.'[21]

The mother and daughter are deeply, unknowingly, connected via these images of nightmare which emphasise a common female hatred of the orthodox polarity that designates the male as active predator and the female as prey to things that 'rush' and things that 'swell'. Both are searching for sexual rhythms in life that are other than mere animal pouncing, and both represent Katherine Mansfield's understanding of women's response to the convention of sexuality that declare this predation typical and necessary.

Linda, unlike Kezia, is alredy trapped in her life. Katherine Mansfield makes her a classic portrait of the condition and response of a Victorian wife and mother to the sexual configurations of her age. Linda is perhaps best seen alongside Mrs Ramsay in Virginia Woolf's *To the Lighthouse* who responds to unsatisfactory elements in her life by encouraging others to recreate them, and in so doing vindicate her own errors. Linda, in 'Prelude', is more shocking in that her unhappiness leaves no room for others and in that the simplicity and directness of Katherine Mansfield's presentation of her allows for no misreading. Her mental disturbance is obvious, as is her incapacity to deal with her world. If Linda's distress has not yet driven her to quite the degree of madness linked with sexual subservience portrayed in Charlotte Perkins Gilman's *The Yellow Wallpaper*, complete breakdown as a direct outcome of unauthentic feminine behaviour is not excluded. The factors that go into making up Linda's condition are easy to identify: she cannot accept her life but neither does she revolt against it; her situation is outside her control; her body is not her own; her feelings exist outside conscious conventions and she can scarcely bear to realise them herself, much less communicate them to a husband who, from what we know about him, could not comprehend a response outside the safety of stereotype, and who would ignore it if he could.

Linda quickly suppresses the truth she has recognised when she finds hatred among her more positive attitudes to her husband. She laughs and thinks,

> why this mania of hers to keep alive at all? . . . What am I guarding myself for so preciously? I shall go on having children and Stanley will go on making money and the children and the gardens will grow bigger and bigger, with whole fleets of aloes in them for me to choose from.[22]

Superficially, a commonsense response which makes light of her danger, and attempts to find delight in the multiplication of life, Linda's rationalisation is, on another level, deeply perverse. Rather than turn her hatred of attack into action, Linda embraces it – embraces that is, death itself and the union of sexuality and death. The children, like the horrid bird, will grow without her love or consent; her egotistical husband will remain unaware of her distress and discontent; and the money that will also grow will be part of the obscene equation. Sex, cash and death will create 'whole fleets of aloes', spiked emblems of hatred binding the woman whose mask will remain in place.

The triumph in 'Prelude', and the sign of the possibility that things might be otherwise, is in the narration which sees and knows and represents what the characters themselves cannot confront. It moves finally to a great distance from the characters who are obliquely summed up in the calico cat with the lid of a cold cream jar over its ear which appears at the end of the story–a final ironic image of the grotesque juncture between culture and natural possibility. Kezia, the potentially free subject, who represents the prospect for another sort of life, tiptoes away in shame at revealing the cat to itself, and in apprehension that she may be found out for breaking the lid–a sign of established cultural codes–which falls to the floor but in fact remains intact. The girl at the end of the story is a sign of the author, challenging the permanency of the world she has described. The lid does not break, but Kezia has seen the cat in the mirror that her mother cannot even bear to look into; there is a possibility that the girl will not lose her vision, that someday the lid *will* break.

'Prelude' is very far from being the simple evocation of childhood memories that it is sometimes taken for. The story is one of Katherine Mansfield's most impressive statements about human relationships and human possibilities, and it revolves around the Burnells' destructive marriage that turns the pastoral setting of the story into a battlefield for a sexual guerrilla war, scarcely apprehended by the maimed combatants for what it is.

Chapter Four

Late Fiction

During the last five years of her life Katherine Mansfield was dying, and for much of that time she knew it. Her literary production during this period was extremely high in volume and in quality, and her *Journal* records a pressing desire to write as much as she could as a means to combat her growing isolation. The letters as well as the *Journal* during this time exhibit a constant attention to the origins of her fiction, and also record Katherine Mansfield's sense of her art as the last area of freedom left in her life. In these letters she makes an important analogy between her writing and the work of the impressionist and post-impressionist painters as both being concerned with a freeing of the imagination from entrenched forms. Manet, Renoir and Cezanne are all sympathetically mentioned, and in a particularly in-teresting letter in 1921 to Dorothy Brett (herself a painter) Katherine Mansfield reminisces about the importance to her of seeing a Van Gogh at the First Post-Impressionist Exhibition in 1910:

Wasn't that Van Gogh shown at the Goupil ten years ago?
Yellow flowers, brimming with sun, in a pot? I wonder if it
is the same. That picture seemed to reveal something I
hadn't realized before I saw it. It lived with me afterwards.
It still does. That and another of a sea-captain in a flat cap.
They taught me something about writing, which was
queer, a kind of freedom – or rather, a shaking free.[1]

The 'shaking free' she mentions here ties in with
another, earlier statement, this time to Murry in 1918,
in which Katherine Mansfield tried to describe the
impetus behind her work. 'I've got two "kick offs" in the
writing game,' she wrote:

> *One* is joy . . . that sort of writing I could only do in just that
> state of being in some perfectly blissful way *at peace*. Then
> something delicate and lovely seems to open before my
> eyes, like a flower without thought of a frost or a cold
> breath – knowing that all about it is warm and tender and
> 'ready'. And *that* I try, ever so humbly, to express.
>
> The other 'kick off' is my old original one, and (had I not
> known love) it would have been my all. Not hate or
> destruction (both are beneath contempt as real motives)
> but an *extremely* deep sense of hopelessness, of everything
> doomed to disaster, almost wilfully, stupidly . . . There! as I
> took out a cigarette paper I got it exactly – *a cry against
> corruption* – that is *absolutely* the nail on the head. Not a
> protest – *a cry*, and I mean corruption in the widest sense of
> the word, of course.[2]

Both of these stated and contrary motives are evident in
the late fiction, with its characteristic moments of
wonder at seeing the world in new and surprising ways,
and in its underlying disgust with entrenched forms. But
the second motive, Katherine Mansfield's original 'kick
off', '*a cry against corruption*', is by far the more important,
and provides the impetus for positing new descriptions
of 'joy', especially in the late fiction, where Katherine

Mansfield's capacity to invent images of post-expressionist vividness and originality surpasses that of any earlier period in her writing.

In the late stories Katherine Mansfield's analysis of gender remains the central instance of her presentation of corruption, which becomes increasingly angry and at times despairing. The characters' masks become heavier. The women characters suffer most, in bodies and rooms and clothes and houses and, ultimately, minds, that are tantamount to prisons. They are hopeless in their seeming powerlessness, unable to assert the autonomy that would also destroy the only identities that they are certain they possess. They continue to be open to various kinds of predation by men that Katherine Mansfield habitually describes as assault. But the men suffer too, from brutalisation of character and false suppression of vulnerability that makes them animals on one hand and emotionally stunted on the other. Under such conditions, word and gesture fail. Katherine Mansfield sees the orthodox pattern of sexual dominance and submission as itself corrupt – when a women character is drawn as dominant, even momentarily, cruelty and distortion are still the operative issues. Sexually, one devours or is devoured. Katherine Mansfield's vision becomes a kind of Darwinian sexual nightmare, a naturalistic view of life that nevertheless denies its inevitability by pointing always to a different order of values signalled by the antagonism of the writing.

The play of the unconscious, too, is given an even bigger part in the late writing, with the self progressively seen as not only fragmented but unknowable. If Katherine Mansfield stresses the mystery of the self *to* the self, a concomitant point is that its inpenetrability to others becomes almost insuperable. Dialogue is seen more and more as a crude and blind gesture across an abyss from one masked and terrified individual to another. And yet the writing, working with the same linguistic tools, strains to reveal that which in the fictional world is portrayed as hidden. For all these reasons, Katherine Mansfield's late writing is profoundly interesting, and the small selection of stories treated here can only provide a suggestion of its power and range.

'Je ne parle pas français' and 'Bliss' were written early in 1918, and both register blazing indictments against the sexual mores and opinions of the time. These stories also attempt to devise new ways to represent sexual pleasure and the vagaries of desire that brand both traditional and contemporary 'progressive' views on the subject as inadequate and inimical to understanding.

Katherine Mansfield thought that 'Je ne parle pas français' marked an epoch in her development as a writer. As she finished it she wrote to Murry saying: 'I don't want to exaggerate the importance of this story or to harp upon it . . . But what I felt so seriously as I wrote it was – ah! I am in a way *grown up* as a writer – a sort of authority.' The next day she wrote about it with similar confidence: 'I *did* feel (I do) that this story is the real thing and that I did not once (as far as I know) shirk it.'[3]

· The excellence of the story lies in its narrative in which the central character is the only direct source of information. The conventions of fiction typically make such a character a locus of sympathy for the reader. Katherine Mansfield plays this convention against itself, denying the inevitability of the correspondence between self-revelation and identification of the reader with the self that is revealed. That she was able to do so had great implications for the status of the reader, and it is scarcely surprising that most of Katherine Mansfield's critics have had difficulties with coming to terms with this story which has probably been the most clumsily read of all her fiction.[4]

'*Je ne parle pas français*' is a brilliantly rendered monologue which reveals the central, corrupted consciousness of Raoul Duquette – gigolo, pimp, *poseur*, artist *manqué* and bisexual fraud – a veritable social monster and a master of contradictions. As he sits in a café, watching the customers, prostitutes and workmen who verify his own feelings of superiority, he recalls his adventure with an English couple and the amusement he derived from the failure of their elopement. Mixed with his pleasure is a seemingly casual attempt at self-justification for his part in the couple's drama. The hidden, but truly revealing theme of his memories is his regret at his failure to exploit sufficiently either the man, Dick Harmon, or the woman, Mouse. Regret, insists Duquette, is an indulgence he never claims: 'I have made it a rule of my life never to regret and never to look back.'[5] But the story is about the pressure of the past on the present and it is deeply concerned with regret – Duquette's regret at losing two particularly enticing victims; the regret of Dick and Mouse at the failure of love; and the angry regret of the governing intelligence of the story on the state of the world it analyses.

Like many modernist works, the time-scheme of the story is convoluted, flickering from the present, to the childhood of Duquette, to the middle-distance of memory. Each level of personal history is tainted by the corruption that culminates in Duquette's narrative itself.

Duquette presents himself as a victim. Repeatedly molested as a child by a laundress, and bribed with cakes for his silence, he has grown into a languid egoist who fancies himself a realist, man of the world and 'first-rate' mind. He dubs his perversity the mark of an artist. Any action, he feels, is permitted to him so long as he has the power to 'feel' intensely, and this is precisely the power he fears he now lacks. In Duquette, Katherine Mansfield attacks a familiar view of the artist as an impresario of the emotions, and condemns it in her delineation of his moral bankruptcy.

Duquette is the complete charlatan. Launching himself as a serious writer he decides that his subject will be the sexual underworld: 'the submerged world. But not as others have done before me. Oh no! Very naively, with a sort of tender humour and from the inside, as though it were all quite simple, quite natural.'⁶ This is, of course, what Duquette is giving us in his monologue but with effects other than those he intends. This self-appointed chronicler of tender degradation first meets Harmon at a fashionable Parisian literary party and begins his assault on him – sending him a copy of his aptly titled book, *False Coins*, and telling him about his own 'submerged' life. Duquette at first marks the Englishman as one of his own kind and is highly surprised when Harmon produces a photo of his mother, 'Dark, handsome, wild-looking, but so full in every line of a kind of haggard pride.'⁷ Duquette revises his reading of Harmon (though Harmon actually *has* shown the Frenchman a talisman of his 'submerged' life), decides he is a highly desirable social and sexual target, and compares his disappointment when he finds Harmon has left Paris to that of a frustrated fox-terrier.

Harmon soon returns and asks Duquette to engage rooms for himself and a woman. On the day of their arrival the Parisian invents two literary successes for himself (a serial, *Wrong Doors*, and a book of poems, *Lost Umbrellas*). At the station, Harmon, distraught, looks like his mother, 'haggard and wild and proud', while the

woman, left behind to tend to the luggage, looks, to
Duquette's astonishment, like a baby. Carrying a grey,
furry muff that she strokes constantly, Mouse's first
words to him are a statement of incapacity –' "*Je ne parle
pas français*" '. Duquette is puzzled and observes Mouse in
the taxi that takes all three to the hotel.

> For Mouse was beautiful. She was exquisite, but so fragile
> and fine that each time I looked at her it was as if for the
> first time . . . She had dark hair and blue or black eyes . . . She
> wore a long dark cloak . . . Where her arms came out of it
> there was grey fur–fur round her neck too, and her close-
> fitting cap was furry.
>   'Carrying out the mouse idea,' I decided.[8]

At the hotel, Mouse makes tea with quiet desperation
while Harmon unaccountably leaves to post a letter. In
fact, he posts himself. The letter he does write is left for
Mouse:

> 'MOUSE, MY LITTLE MOUSE,
>   It's no good. It's impossible. I can't see it through. Oh, I do
> love you. I do love you Mouse, but I can't hurt her. People
> have been hurting her all her life. I simply dare not give her
> this final blow. You see, though she's stronger than both of
> us, she's so frail and proud. It would kill her – kill her Mouse.
> And, oh God, I can't kill my mother! . . . '[9]

Astounded again, Duquette is also fascinated as Mouse's
tears fall: 'With her eyes shut, with her face quite calm
except for the quivering eyelids. The tears pearled down
her cheeks and she let them fall.'[10] Stranded, with only a
little money, at once too frightened and too dignified to
pursue Harmond, unable to go back because '"all my
friends think I'm married,"' Mouse is left in Duquette's

hands. He too abandons her. As he leaves the hotel he realises: 'Why they were suffering . . . these two . . . really suffering. I have seen two people suffer as I don't suppose I ever shall again . . . ' The connoisseur of 'feeling' feels nothing but surprise at its existence. In the café, safely buffered by time, Duquette fantasises about what he could have done with Mouse – pimped for her, kept her for himself, overseen the destruction of an innocence he is not likely to encounter again. Even he cannot understand why he walked away:

> Even now I don't fully understand why. Of course, I knew I couldn't have kept it up. That had a great deal to do with it. But you would have though, putting it at its lowest, curiosity couldn't have kept my fox-terrier nose away . . .
> *Je ne parle pas français*. That was her swan song for me.[11]

The *'français'* that Mouse does not speak is the 'language' of corruption, egoism and of the stated valuing of emotional sensation that in fact fears it. It is a language that Duquette speaks to perfection, that Harmon, with his incestuous leanings and need to avoid adult autonomy by remaining his mother's child, also knows. Dick Harmon, like his namesake John Harmon in Dickens's *Our Mutual Friend*, which Katherine Mansfield read with admiration as she wrote '*Je ne parle pas français*',[12] is a man travelling in disguise, his capacity for love governed by another's 'will'. Mouse, an image of women as prey, is the ultimate victim, a vulnerable, furry morsel for any 'fox-terrier'. She is perfectly isolated, simply left behind like one of the lost umbrellas in Duquette's spurious book. Mouse is suspended in the narrative, eternally weeping, eternally betrayed in a world in which all but she are initiated into a duplicitous language of desire. She is triply open to attack: by Harmon, who promises a love he cannot deliver; by Duquette, who finds her fragility an invitation to despoliation. Finally, Mouse is self-endangered by her acquiescence to a tradition of feminine honour and feminine passivity expressed in her mouse disguise, her name and her remark about marriage.

The success of the story lies not only in the evocation of evil from the inside (Katherine Mansfield is doing in prose in this story something akin to what Robert Browning did in poetry in *The Ring and the Book*), but also in the multiple readings the tale will bear. From one point of view, the story is one in which traditional maidenly innocence inexplicably stays the hand of radical malevolence. From another, this innocence does not triumph, it is simply abandoned in a world where it is useless. Mouse's innocence is a colluding factor in her suffering. Her unexamined trust of her lover leads to a disaster that invalidates all the patterns of life she knows. From another point of view this is a story about inescapable victimisation and universal warping of desire – Duquette's by the laundress, Harmon's by his mother, Mouse's by the men and by the mask of her feminine role–that generates more victimisation and deformation in turn. In all these views love is either thwarted or irrelevant, and suffering and betrayal are the central facts of experience. Each character is painfully static. Only the reader sees enough to understand the evil of their situation and the only voice heard is that of Duquette, the voice of the world itself, insulating itself from an emotional response to its circumstances.

Finally, the story is most decidedly an attack on a view of art in which, like Duquette, the artist substitutes sexual 'sophistication' for moral judgement. There is a clear hierarchy of condemnation in the story, with the

woman as the ultimate prey of the evil that congests the
social patterns of which the story speaks.

In 'Bliss', Katherine Mansfield again challenges contemporary views regarding sexual sophistication at the
same time as she tries to invent a new way to write about
the awakening of female desire. Her views on the subject
are extremely interesting, and accounts of her 'priggish-
ness' in declining to write explicitly about sexual
intercourse in her fiction have completely misconstrued
the nature of her objections.

In this matter, Katherine Mansfield's views ran
counter to her era, during which the familiar, and by
now almost obligatory twentieth-century vocabulary of
sexual response in fiction was being devised. In 1920,
during the time she worked steadily as a reviewer of
contemporary fiction for the *Athenaeum* under Murry's
editorship, she announced her disgust with the growth
of a particular kind of explicit eroticism in fiction by
women writers:

> I don't know whether it's I that have 'fallen behind' in this
> procession but truly the books I read nowadays astound me.
> Female writers discovering a freedom, a frankness, a
> licence, to speak their hearts, reveal themselves as . . . sex
> maniacs. There's not one relationship between a man and a
> woman that isn't the one sexual relationship – at its lowest.
> Intimacy is the sexual act. I am terribly ashamed to tell the
> truth; it's a very horrible exposure.[13]

It is not only women authors who prompt this response;
Katherine Mansfield criticises both Joyce and Lawrence
for the same reason. For example, she complains that the
characters in Lawrence's *The Lost Girl* are merely 'animals
on the prowl . . . they submit to physical response and for

the rest go veiled–blind–*faceless–mindless*. This is the doctrine of mindlessness.'[14]

In talking about sexual response herself, Katherine Mansfield works closely to the conventions of obliqueness that characterised nineteenth-century fiction-conventions of metaphor and symbolic suggestion that point to the inextricability of body and mind in desire, rather than adopting the twentieth-century 'empirical' conventions that represent sexual activity as a collision of bodies – mechanical and unproblematic occasions for the manufacture of 'natural', physiological pleasure. Katherine Mansfield understood very clearly that the ideas behind these new conventions were extremely suspect, that they meant, as Stephen Heath puts it in *The Sexual Fix*, 'not liberation but a myth, an ideology, the definition of a new mode of conformity'[15] which contained as many unacceptable and unexamined implications for women as more recognisably traditional notions of women's sexual blankness or rapaciousness. This does not mean that Katherine Mansfield was not interested in the subject, she would scarcely belong to this century if she were not. But the *kind* of account she gives of desire works in a different direction to that of most other modernist writers.

'Bliss' takes account of the impact of socially dictated patterns which structure the individual's conception of what should legitimately satisfy desire, and enacts the wonder and distress that follows from an awakening to the insufficiency of those definitions. Katherine Mansfield sees desire as diffuse and unpredictable, and in the story shows her awareness of the fine mesh of social definition that is supposed to contain, express and control the desires of an advanced, western woman.

It is because of this social theme that 'Bliss' is crowded with people, in this case members of a smart London arty set, the kind of sophisticated social group that Katherine Mansfield often pilloried. The bantering cleverness of her satire of the set – Mrs Norman Knight, with her coat patterned with monkeys, plays crudely for shock value; Eddie Warren enthuses about a line in the latest poem in the latest review: '"Why Must it Always be Tomato Soup?" ' – gives a representation in the narrative of the pretensions it mocks. The group is wrapped in conventions, though it takes itself to be frightfully liberated and knowing.

Liberation and knowledge are exactly what are in question for Bertha Young, the thirty-year-old hostess of the party that takes place in the story and whose consciousness is reflected in the writing. As far as she consciously knows, she has everything she has been told she could want:

> She was young. Harry and she were as much in love as ever, and they got on splendidly and were really good pals. She had an adorable baby. They didn't have to worry about money. They had this absolutely satisfactory house and garden. And friends – modern thrilling friends, writers and painters and poets and people keen on social questions – just the kind of friends they wanted. And then there were books, and there was music, and she had found a wonderful little dressmaker, and they were going abroad in the summer and their new cook made the most superb omelettes . . . [16]

As she consciously rifles through her assets, Bertha tries hard to find the item that will 'prove' to herself she is happy. The barely suppressible waves of emotion that Bertha identifies as 'bliss' at the opening of the story are really signs of the hysteria that threatens to overcome her and that negates her conviction of well-being. She feels that this 'bliss', despite her modern 'freedom', is something she must hide:

> Oh, is there no way you can express it without being 'drunk and disorderly?' How idiotic civilisation is! Why be given a body if you have to keep it shut up in a case like a rare, rare fiddle?[17]

The story makes it clear that Bertha is caught between two 'civilised' conventions of female desire – the convention that outlaws women's physicality as taboo and unnatural, and, on the other hand, the alternative 'modern' convention that speaks endlessly of desire, defining it and channelling it into patterns that may not accord with individual experience. Even though Bertha's life is supposedly so free, it is, in fact, arranged so that she is restrained from physical contacts of all kinds, though the *talk* about such satisfactions is endless. The result is that the physical contacts she does make electrify her.

Katherine Mansfield deploys various emblems of female sexuality through the story and shows Bertha responding to them. Arranging bowls of fruit becomes such a sensuous activity that Bertha can hardly control herself. Being allowed to feed her baby, who is really 'mothered' by a nurse, pushes her again to the brink of hysteria. As much in control of the imagery as in 'Prelude', Katherine Mansfield provides the analogues to the danger of sensuous response that so torments Bertha in images of the 'wild' life of the animals and plants that persist in their elemental forms in the city. Even in Bertha's bright modern world, in which consciousness is supposed to have banished secrets, there is her garden, full of its own life in the dusk of her psyche:

At the far end, against the wall, there was a tall, slender pear tree in the fullest, richest bloom; it stood perfect, as though becalmed against the jade-green sky. Bertha couldn't help feeling, even from this distance, that it had not a single bud or faded petal. Down below, in the garden beds, the red and yellow tulips, heavy with flowers, seemed to lean upon the dusk. A grey cat, dragging its belly, crept across the lawn, and a black one, its shadow, trailed after. The sight of them, so intent and quick, gave Bertha a curious shudder.[18]

Bertha attempts a 'modern' reaction to the scene. '"What a creepy thing cats are!" she stammered.' The garden, with its flaming Blakean pear tree, heavy Rubensesque tulips and Lawrencian cats, is redolent with sexual suggestion for Bertha, who only unconsciously registers her response to the scene. The image is well chosen. The walled garden itself has been a classic image for unawakened female sexuality since the Middle Ages: here it works as a feature of Bertha's ordinary landscape that suddenly explodes into meaning for her. Katherine Mansfield makes all these associations work in this metaphorical garden of the unawakened woman. The paradox is that Bertha's 'fast' set bases its swagger on its freedom regarding sexual matters. Bertha's acquiescence to these mores is, then, radically fraudulent, though she does not know this. Everything she is is based on a lack of knowledge.

Bertha dresses for her party in the colours of her garden, the bridal colours of white and green of the pear tree and the sky. If Bertha is dressed as a bride, her most interesting guest, Pearl Fulton, is dressed in the silvery, pearly colours of the moon, echoing primitive connections between the moon and full female sexuality.[19] While the dinner guests jabber on ('"Isn't she very *liée* with Michael Oat?" "The man who wrote *Love in False*

Teeth?"'), Bertha feels herself in sudden, wordless intimacy with Pearl who surveys the scene indirectly through 'heavy eyelids'. Her bedroom eyes and bedroom manner work powerfully on Bertha who is pulled toward her. Again the 'bliss' returns and Bertha looks for a sign that Pearl has also felt the disturbing link between them. Bertha tries to account for her feelings: 'I believe this does happen very, very rarely between women. Never between men,' she thinks while looking again for a sign from the first adult object of her newly awakened but misunderstood desire. Pearl gives the sign. She asks to see Bertha's garden.

> 'Have you a garden?' said the cool, sleepy voice.
> This was so exquisite on her part that all Bertha could do was to obey. She crossed the room, pulled the curtains apart, and opened those long windows.
> 'There!' she breathed.
> And the two women stood side by side looking at the slender flowering tree. Although it was so still it seemed, like the flame of a candle, to stretch up, to point, to quiver in the bright air, to grow taller and taller as they gazed – almost to touch the rim of the round, silver moon.
> How long did they stand there? Both, as it were, caught in that circle of unearthly light, understanding each other perfectly, creatures of another world, and wondering what they were to do in this one with all this blissful treasure that burned in their bosoms, and dropped, in silver flowers, from their hair and hands.[20]

Or so Bertha interprets their communion. The reader, of course, is meant to see things differently. While Bertha dramatically reveals the garden of her sexual potential in triumph to a creature who has finally become the focus for her crystallised desire in a way that Bertha herself does not understand, she does not know that she is standing with a woman who is already

emblematically identified with the full moon high above
the garden, and already in her own communion with the
phallic implications of the pear tree which Bertha
disregards, but which are also a part of its significance.
Symbolically, both women are bathed in the light of the
moon of female sexuality, but Pearl already *is* the moon;
Bertha is merely the guardian of a garden, hidden behind
windows and curtains, stunned by the moon's light.

Bertha's free-flowing sexual response moves from
Pearl to her own husband. For the first time she desires
him. As she takes cognisance of this amazing new
sensation, she identifies the source of the 'bliss' she has
been fighting back. And as she looks around to take
possession of him when the guests leave, she sees him
kissing Pearl. They are lovers. She understands that she
has discovered her sexuality only in time to see its first
two objects already in full possession of the pleasure she
is only on the threshold of knowing. Bertha is left alone,
on the edge of an abyss, her bliss turned to dismay, and
with the pear tree, bisexual emblem of her just
discovered sexual need, 'as lovely as ever and as full of
flower and as still.'[21]

The ending is one of absolute and bleak exclusion; the
outlets for Bertha's belated sexual flowering are
suddenly blocked; a possibility is left senseless and dead
in her hands. Katherine Mansfield's simultaneous
control of a Jazz Age story as characteristic of the period
as F. Scott Fitzgerald's, and of a deep structure drawing
on a pattern of images that effortlessly shapes the story
demonstrates the power of her late technique. The
symbols are selected and placed with great tact and
evocativeness, suggesting their multiple meanings
without ever insisting on them. (For example, Pearl is
associated with the moon but also with the grey cat
dragging its belly through Bertha's walled garden, her

sexuality seen as both utterly transcendent and utterly sordid. At the same time the moon and the cat are both functions of Bertha's unconscious, overdetermined in their meaning by her heightened emotional state.) But the most telling aspect of the story is the ending, with Bertha pushed from the chatter of her self-consciously modern, sophisticated life into the internal crisis whose source she has just discovered and whose cure was theoretically within her reach until the moment she was ready to grasp it.

The double structure of symbol and social critique provides two axes along which Katherine Mansfield can make her observations about the cultural base of women's psychology. Modern assumptions about sex are indirectly shown to be ill-suited to understanding the waywardness and unpredictability of individual response. The 'advanced' notions of the 'Bliss' clique are as useless as the more traditional orthodoxy operative in most of the other stories. The ethical undertones of the story are still more complex. 'Bliss' not only raises difficult questions about loyalties inside and outside of marriage and that place that sexuality holds within it, but also about the kind of freedom enacted as self-serving practice. Betrayed by both male and female, and part of a set that would not recognise Pearl and Harry's affair as betrayal at all, Bertha's distress must be masked by the hypocrisy of a social posture of openness. Superficial poses of freedom lead here to inauthenticity as surely as surfaces of repression do. The group still closes ranks against the outsider. Bertha is a victim of a psychological game she had no conscious idea she was playing.

If Katherine Mansfield's stories about women psychologically alone in the smart sets of London and New

Zealand are painful, those written about women left outside the protective screens of men, money and class are often devastating in their emotional impact. Along with her contemporary, Jean Rhys, Katherine Mansfield has a reputation for her stories of the *femme seule*, and many of her late stories fit into this category. This subgenre is in many ways a continuation of the nineteenth-century 'governess' novel – we are close to the conventions of *Jane Eyre* here – with the change that there is no hope for a happy ending, no matter how qualified, no chance that the excluded woman will be fitted back, on any terms, into the relationships that are meant to define and enclose her life.

Katherine Mansfield's 'Miss Brill', written in 1920, is probably her most famous sketch of a woman alone. As she explained in a letter, she worked to put the story together in terms of 'a musical composition – trying to get it nearer and nearer to the expression of Miss Brill – until it fitted her'.[22] Once again, Katherine Mansfield's mature narrative method operates in the story as the writing strives to convey the experience of Miss Brill through the presentation of events in the vocabulary and cadences of her mind.

'Miss Brill' is the loneliest of all of Katherine Mansfield's stories about lonely women. It is sometimes compared with James Joyce's 'Clay',[23] but is different in tone, in its ultimate significance, and in its impression of participation in the miseries of the woman's consciousness which is portrayed. Like Joyce's little laundress, so extravagantly willing to be pleased by a world that gives her little but hard knocks, Miss Brill is eager to be part of a scene that ruthlessly excludes her. But whereas in the *Dubliners* story we are asked to pity Maria, and we are not sure of the extent to which she absorbs the humiliation we so painfully see, in 'Miss Brill' the reader is more closely implicated, both with the character and with the world, as we are made to watch the character take the full force of the transformation of her consciousness of herself from participant to exile. It is a cruel process, and Katherine Mansfield refuses to temper any detail of its typicality.

Miss Brill lives alone in France, patching together an income from scraps of English teaching and from reading the newspaper to an invalid. She keeps herself going by reining her expectations in tightly with a chirpy, inconsequentiality of mind and with her conformity to a tattered notion of gentility. Her surroundings smack of the deprivation of a lone woman – a dark little room, her meagre treat of a honey-cake which she looks forward to each week as her only self-indulgence. She most significantly identifies herself with her furpiece, a decayed thing she keeps in a box under her bed, and which represents to her all the luxury and adventure in life that she convinces herself she shares. She values, too, the sensuality and flirtatiousness of the fur, itself an emblem of the traditional man-fascinating ways out of poverty for a woman that she still obliquely believes apply to herself. But the fur, her only friend, is not what it used to be; even Miss Brill can see that.

> Dear little thing! It was nice to feel it again. She had taken it out of its box that afternoon, shaken out the moth-powder, given it a good brush, and rubbed the life back into the dim little eyes . . . But the nose, which was of some black composition, wasn't really at all firm . . . Little rogue! Yes, she really felt like that about it. Little rogue biting its tail just by her left ear.[24]

The lonely woman feels herself as roguish as her fur as she slips out to the public concert which is her Sunday entertainment. For her, the afternoon in the park is concert and theatre combined, for she feels herself part of a complex drama as she watches the other concertgoers from her bench. She prides herself on her understanding of life and her ability to interpret strangers' affairs from a distance. But her keenest pleasure is in eavesdropping, and at first she is disappointed, as a woman starved for words, with the silent old couple sharing her bench. When a pair of young lovers replace them she is delighted; she loves lovers, they are an unexpected treat. She sees them as the hero and heroine in a thrilling drama she directs and in which she participates. Smiling, she listens to their conversation:

'No, not now,' said the girl. 'Not here, I can't.'
'But why? Because of that stupid old thing at the end there?' asked the boy. 'Why does she come here at all – who wants her? Why doesn't she keep her silly old mug at home?'
'It's her fu-fur which is so funny,' giggled the girl. 'It's exactly like a fried whiting.'[25]

Miss Brill drags herself back to 'her room like a cupboard' and, without looking, puts the fur into its box. 'But when she put the lid on she thought she heard something crying'.[26] The extraordinary pathos of the story and of Miss Brill herself derives from the depth of the central character's courage and self-control which is nevertheless expended in acquiescence to a view of a woman's function that is bound to abase her. The story portrays a consciousness distancing itself from its own suffering isolation with a tremendous degree of pain and yet with a dignity that is in itself a kind of virtue. Miss Brill is written off as a horror by a code that condemns her on the grounds of sex, age, beauty, poverty and singleness, the same code that Miss Brill herself uses to explain her disappointment with the old couple on the beach and which now comes full circle to indict her as less than human. This is a portrait of a woman caught by the contradictions of social preconceptions that she herself has internalised. What Miss Brill stuffs into the box under the lonely bed of the *femme seule* is, according to the logic of the image, herself.

The early 1920s were the culminating years for literary modernism in English. Pound's *Mauberley* came out in 1920; Lawrence's *Women in Love* and Richardson's *Deadlock* in 1921; Eliot's *Waste Land*, Joyce's *Ulysses*, Yeats's *Later Poems* and Woolf's *Jacob's Room* in 1922. 1921 was the *annus mirabilis* for Katherine Mansfield's later work, during which she produced a crop of brilliant stories that themselves provide a review of all the concerns which had shaped her fiction and which extend her treatment of them through the application of her late technical subtlety.

The overriding interest in the stories of 1921 remains the unpredictability of the self and the impossibility of direct communication between individuals. Katherine Mansfield stressed this point again in 1922, when, in a letter to Murry, she insists on her familiar preoccupation: 'We are all hidden, looking out at each other; I mean even those of us who want not to hide.'[27]

Moments of connection, much less communication, are rare in Katherine Mansfield's work, but in 'At the Bay' (1921), one of the Burnell stories, she provides accounts of several moments when the barriers between her characters break down. Like 'Prelude', 'At the Bay' is an impressionistic story held together by running motifs of animal images and of varieties of symbolic response to the sea.[28]

'At the Bay' has a pastoral opening, patterned by images that embody the characters, their actions, their deficiencies and the mysterious influences that work upon them. The scene set is primal, an alternative Genesis: the sea is divided from the safety of the land, a flock of sheep and a wise old shepherd with his dog appears, a rebellious cat surveys the controlled, domestic animals with disdain, a huge gum-tree spreads its arms over the whole of the scene. Against the background of these 'timeless' images, the Burnells go into action, locked in roles that are fixed by their historical moment. Stanley plays his usual role of macho buffoon, beginning his day with an officious encounter with his brother-in-law, Jonathan, during his morning dip. It is all that Stanley can do with the possibilities of the unconscious which the sea, in the story, represents. The prose moves from the lyricism of the opening images to the self-important bluster of Stanley's mind, and it stays in this register until the women of the family bundle him into the coach for work. As he leaves, the whole house relaxes, with the narrative catching the change from the women's tension to their harmony in relief at his departure. Even Beryl, still driven by her lack of success in ensnaring a husband, and still engaged in a nervous flirtation with Stanley, is glad to see him go:

> 'Good-bye, Stanley', called Beryl, sweetly and gaily. It was easy enough to say good-bye! And there she stood, idle, shading her eyes with her hand. The worst of it was Stanley had to shout good-bye too, for the sake of appearances. Then he saw her turn, give a little skip and run back to the house. She was glad to be rid of him!
>
> Yes, she was thankful. Into the living-room she ran and called 'He's gone!' Linda cried from her room: 'Beryl! Has Stanley gone?' Old Mrs. Fairfield appeared, carrying the boy in his little flannel coatee.
>
> 'Gone?'
>
> 'Gone!'
>
> Oh, the relief, the difference it made to have the man out

of the house. Their very voices changed as they called to one another; they sounded warm and loving and as if they shared a secret. Beryl went over to the table. 'Have another cup of tea, mother. It's still hot.' She wanted, somehow, to celebrate the fact that they could do what they liked now. There was no man to disturb them; the whole perfect day was theirs.

'No, thank you, child,' said old Mrs. Fairfield, but the way at that moment she tossed the boy up and said 'a-goos-a-goos-a-ga!' to him meant that she felt the same. The little girls ran into the paddock like chickens let out of a coop.

Even Alice, the servant girl, washing up the dishes in the kitchen, caught the infection and used the precious tank water in a perfectly reckless fashion.

'Oh, these men!' said she, and she plunged the teapot into the bowl and held it under the water even after it had stopped bubbling, as if it too was a man and drowning was too good for them.[29]

Katherine Mansfield deftly dramatises the relaxation of the women into mutual kindness as they make their various gestures of relief with the departure of Stanley. The women of all ages and social conditions respond more strongly to their moment of liberation than their external behaviour can indicate, but for an instant they are united in the communal expression of freedom grasped with pleasure.

Another writer concerned with portraying the condition of women might have left it at that: with symbolic Alice symbolically drowning all men in her symbolic sink in her symbolic kitchen while the women move in a harmony of rapture through the house. But Katherine Mansfield's moment of shared release is over in an instant. Alice stays at her sink; Beryl's frustration is not eased. The unity is, after all, only temporary; nothing essential has changed. Once the emotional reflex of relief has passed the characters go their separate ways, their female condition of restraint blending with other facets of their personalities to shape them in the series of duet-like encounters that follow. The little girls run off to play with their cousins; Alice visits a jolly widow happy with her independence (' "freedom's best" ', she tells Alice); Kezia confronts the idea of death in a moving conversation with her grandmother; Linda feels a stab of love for her new son, who, up to this point, has left her only hostile or indifferent, and has a moment of connection with Jonathan.

There are only a few instances in all of Katherine Mansfield's fiction where she suggests what a true meeting between the sexes might entail. The most powerful of these occurs in 'At the Bay' during Linda's conversation with Jonathan. It is important to notice that the fellow feeling in this encounter is only possible because Jonathan falls hopelessly short when measured against standards of orthodox masculine behaviour and success which are typified by Stanley. Linda, as in 'Prelude', is unhappy, still enmeshed in the expectations of her class and era. Jonathan, however, interests her.

> Linda thought again how attractive he was. It was strange to think that he was only an ordinary clerk, that Stanley earned twice as much money as he. What was the matter with Jonathan? He had no ambition; she supposed that was it. And yet one felt he was gifted, exceptional. He was passionately fond of music; every spare penny he had went on books. He was always full of new ideas, schemes, plans. But nothing came of it all. The new fire blazed in Jonathan ... but a moment later it had fallen in and there was nothing but ashes, and Jonathan went around with a look like hunger in his eyes.[30]

Jonathan himself understands what is wrong; he loathes

the half of the sexist equation that defines the worth of a man largely by the money he can make, and yet he realises that his own life has been set in its pattern of unease by the very values he rejects.

> 'It seems to me just as imbecile, just as infernal, to have to go to the office on Monday,' said Jonathan, 'as it always has done and always will do. To spend all the best years of one's life sitting on a stool from nine to five, scratching on someone's ledger! It's a queer use to make of one's . . . one and only life, isn't it?'[31]

Jonathan is kept 'in jail' by his marriage and family. '"I've two boys to provide for," ' he says, but he is wistfully pulled toward a larger life, a world that he sees as a ' "vast dangerous garden, waiting out there, undiscovered, unexplored"'. And it is too late to change. He says, in response to Linda's empathy and sympathy: '"I'm old – I'm old."' He bends his head and to Linda's sad surprise shows the grey speckling his hair. Like Kezia with her grandmother in the same story, the characters bow together before knowledge of mortality; age and sexual differences are brushed aside in recognition of the inevitability of death and in wonder at the fixity of personal history.

This single, moving instance of unmasked connection between a woman and a man emphasises the similarities rather than the divergences in the human condition. The moment depends on the fact that Jonathan is capable of wonder and is intellectually alive, and that Linda is in sympathy with these qualities despite her own choice of bourgeois safety. Even if Jonathan is a failed rebel, it is crucial that his disgust with masculine roles is one of the most significant aspects of his character. Sensitivity and rejection of a totally materialist view of the world point to the ways in which the existential bad faith, which

Katherine Mansfield sees as generally poisoning life, might be overcome. It is, of course, a traditional spiritual and intellectual solution that is offered, but it is a tradition that Katherine Mansfield herself embraces. Yet even in this rare moment of meeting in her fiction, the direct occasion for abandoning roles is the intimate realisation of mortality. The joy in the characters' easiness together is touched by the corruption of death. Katherine Mansfield sees love and death, pity and fellow feeling, and the realisation of human boundaries and possibilities meeting in a solemn and stoic frame.

If sexual *rapprochment* such as that which takes place between Linda and Jonathan is portrayed as possible to characters able to abandon, even momentarily, the divisive effects of social convention (and one must point out that *both* Linda and Jonathan are failures if judged by the standards of social orthodoxy), and see instead the commonality in the human condition, the experiences of Beryl, in her dealings with the Kembers, illustrate the power that the failure to fulfil conventional sexual expectations has to warp all other relationships. In 'Prelude' as well as in 'At the Bay', Beryl is shown in the process of being driven literally mad by her lack of a husband – a case that balances against Linda's equal distress in her marriage. In Beryl, Katherine Mansfield delineates the process that creates the embittered spinster by providing no option in life but marriage for the respectable woman. Attractive, lively Beryl, able to measure her success as a human being only by the acquisition of a man, enraged by her lack of success as an unmarried aunt, emotionally unfulfilled, financially dependent, is caught in the period between hope of changing and despair at the permanency of her condition. She lives chiefly in her divided imagination; the prose that depicts her consciousness is alternately swooning, romantic and fanciful, and angry, violent and tyrannical. Beryl consistently lashes out at the world which, as far as she can see, allows her only one avenue to happiness which she, by herself, can do nothing to secure. Because she lives so much in her own mind, and is absorbed by its contradictions, she does not even see the disastrous nature of her sister's marriage. Marriage to Beryl seems the answer to every problem, including that of the torment of the internal divisions which assail her. Her hysteria (and she is another of Katherine Mansfield's characters likely to lose herself in moments of panicky breakdown) is rooted in her definition as a woman, and her blind need is punctuated by moments of illumination. In 'Prelude', at night, she regards herself in the mirror:

> Oh God, there she was, back again, playing the same old game. False – false as ever . . . False even when she was alone with herself, now . . . .
> 'Oh,' she cried, 'I am so miserable – so frightfully miserable. I know that I'm silly and spiteful and vain; I'm always acting a part. I'm never my real self for a moment.'[32]

Beryl's sense of herself as masked presupposes a different self beneath the mask, waiting for liberation. The narrative, however, does not verify this belief. The mask *is* Beryl, as much as the doubtful and self-critical response to that mask is also a secret part of her identity. But the whole of her discontinuous character has only one function–to save herself from what she sees as her social isolation, her cultural placelessness. In 'At the Bay', since no acceptable attachment presents itself, Beryl turns to the unacceptable Kembers.

Escaping from her mother on the beach, Beryl plunges into the sea with 'fast' Mrs Kember, whose disregard for the proprieties goes further than her cigarettes, her 'lack of vanity, her slang, and the way she treated men as though she was one of them, and the fact that she didn't care twopence about her house'. Katherine Mansfield draws a hard line around the relationship between the two women – the external marks of Mrs Kember's 'liberation' say nothing about her moral quality. In fact, she is a sexual predator as much as the men she so closely imitates. Her lesbian predation of Beryl is emphasised in her parody of male seduction, her leering compliments to Beryl about her body, her 'stolen' caressing touches. Like a 'rat', Mrs Kember leaves Beryl, who plays up to her, feeling as if 'she was being poisoned by this cold woman . . . how strange, how horrible!' But Beryl needs to hear the kind of crude seductive comments Mrs Kember makes, and will listen to her in the absence of any man to make them instead. At the end of the story, she does have her chance at a man. Harry Kember, the equally predatory husband of the rat-woman, calls her into the garden at night. Beryl joins him but ends in running away, leaving the silence and 'the sound of the sea . . . a vague murmur, as though it waked out of a dark dream'.[33] What Katherine Mansfield shows Beryl drawing back from is not Mrs Kember's lesbianism nor Harry Kember's extramarital embrace, but something *both* characters represent. It is the Kember's predation, their being seducers, *victimisers* rather than lovers, that is Katherine Mansfield's concern.

'At the Bay', despite its moments of connection, ends with danger in Beryl's escape from further psychological corrosion. What she flees from is simultaneously her own desire and its fulfilment, and a victimisation that would distortedly enact the marriage she needs for personal validation. The sound of the sea, image of these confusions and possibilities, takes the narrative back to timelessness, and to the chaotic mumblings of dream and desire.

Kezia probably has a less important role in 'At the Bay' than in any of the Burnell stories, but she is once again at the centre of 'The Doll's House' (1921). The little girls in this story, like Nora in the play by Ibsen after which it is named, and like the little girl in 'Pearl Button', are female rebels in revolt against the sexual and social rules that are meant to divide them into hostile and permanently alienated camps. Kezia is the heroine, and the story concerns her breaking her family's injunction against allowing the 'impossible' Kelvey girls to see the Burnells' new doll's house.

Lil and Else Kelvey are the pariahs of the playground. They are poor children who are used by the school and the parents of the other girls as negative object-lessons of what, for females, is beyond the pale. The Kelveys are 'shunned by everybody'.

> They were the daughters of a spry, hard-working little washerwoman, who went about from house to house by the day. This was awful enough. But where was Mr. Kelvey? Nobody knew for certain. But everybody said he was in prison. So they were the daughters of a washerwoman and a gaolbird. Very nice company for other people's children! And they looked it. Why Mrs. Kelvey made them so conspicuous was hard to understand. The truth was they were dressed in 'bits' given to her by the people for whom she worked.[34]

The narrative mimics the tone of the self-righteous, disapproving, genteel community (and these are women's tones, women's voices defending their class territory). Aside from the fundamental class snobbery in operation here, there is an explicit outline of what conformity to female stereotype must mean. Women must not work, they can only be fully validated on the production of a suitable male from whom they ought to derive their status, their being is closely bound up in their clothes. Self-sufficiency, hard work, and cheerful courage (supposedly valued by the same culture) are unacceptable: Mrs Kelvey and her daughters fail on every sexist point.

On a day that the outcasts have been particularly tormented in the schoolyard, Kezia violates her mother's ban on the girls. Seeing them coming down the road she it torn, in a moment reminiscent of Huck Finn's espousal of the 'nigger' Jim, between the social conscience her culture has been developing and an individual stroke of consciousness.

> Nobody was about; she began to swing on the big white gates of the courtyard. Presently, looking along the road, she saw two little dots. They grew bigger, they were coming towards her. Now she could see that one was in front and one close behind. Now she could see that they were the Kelveys. Kezia stopped swinging. She slipped off the gate as if she was going to run away. Then she hesitated. The Kelveys came nearer, and beside them walked their shadows, very long, stretching right across the road with their heads in the buttercups. Kezia clambered back on the gate; she had made up her mind; she swung out.[35]

As in 'Pearl Button' the gate is a sign of vacillation between being shut into or moving out of convention. And again, the central character swings free. Kezia asks the Kelveys in and they have a chance to see the doll's house before Aunt Beryl shoos them off. The shadows of the girls, 'stretching right across the road with their heads in the buttercups', is what decides Kezia to make her move. The delicacy and beauty of the highly original image contrasts strongly with the clipped, factual language of crude perception that records Kezia's sighting of the girls, and the text reflects the shift from the crudity of dispassionate observation to Kezia's sympathetic recognition of the outlaw children. The shadows that merge the little girls with the beauty of the flowers simply ignore the confining man-made road and its straight lines. Kezia does the same as she obliterates the class lines of her acculturation and recognises the Kelveys as in some sense equals. And in doing so, Kezia denies the values their rejection represents.

The doll's house itself is a complex symbol that precisely suits the story. Given to the Burnell girls by Mrs Hay ('Sweet old Mrs Hay', a woman whose bland, rustic, vegetable name connotes her conformity), the doll's house has to be left outside. As Beryl thinks:

> No harm could come to it; it was summer. And perhaps the smell of paint would have gone by the time it had to be taken in. For, really, the smell of paint coming from that doll's house . . . the smell of paint was quite enough to make anyone seriously ill . . . [36]

The doll's house is completely furnished, down to 'the father and mother dolls, who . . . were really too big for the doll's house',[37] just as real people are 'too big' for the kind of married life that the doll's house metonymically represents. Even when new, the doll's house smells revolting, like the institution it imitates. And just as the Kelveys are used as a negative lesson for the Burnell girls, the doll's house is meant for positive female instruction. It is an invitation to sweet domesticity, to boast about possessions; it provides an opportunity for a complete childish parody of the approved method for women to locate their identities in their houses and in the things and people they manage to stuff into them. But the doll's house is also a fabulous toy, a playground for the wayward imagination, and it contains one item that particularly catches Kezia's fancy: a tiny lamp that almost looks as if it could be lit. Katherine Mansfield once more uses the classic association of lamps and knowledge to indicate the rebelliousness of Kezia's reaction to the house. Although the lamp is false, as is the system of values embodied by the house and summed up in the persecution of the Kelveys, it is the *idea* of the lamp that catches Kezia's attention. The linkage of Kezia and the Kelveys earlier in the story is repeated via the mediation of this image. Else nudges Lil at the very end of the story: 'she smiled her rare smile.'I seen the little lamp," she said softly. Then both were silent once more.'[38] The image unites the girl-children, the outcast and the privileged, in their imaginations which refuse the patterns dictated by their culture and create alternative patterns of their own.

Three more stories of 1921 need to be taken into account before ending this study of Katherine Mansfield's fiction: 'The Garden-Party', 'The Daughters of the Late Colonel', and 'Life of Ma Parker'. These stories, along with 'Miss Brill' and 'At the Bay', were collected in *The Garden-Party* (1922), the last of the three volumes of stories that Katherine Mansfield published during her life. All three are stories about mortality, particularly women's consciousness of mortality, and I can think of no other woman writer, with the exception of Emily Dickinson, who gives the subject such close attention. For all that has been made of the connection between Katherine Mansfield's own awareness of impending death at this time, it is necessary to note that her interest in the subject in her writing of 1921 was concentrated on the effect of death on the living, and it adds another dimension to her consistent portraiture of women's isolation and exclusion.

'The Garden-Party' is a case in point. As in 'Bliss', Katherine Mansfield sets up a situation in which a woman is suddenly displaced from a frenetic social whirl that supposedly defines the totality of her being. The Sheridans in the story are a variant of the Burnells; the setting is New Zealand and the characters prototypical colonials.

The Sheridan children, all young adults, are giving a party. The excited, happy narrative sees what they see in the terms that they see it – their fine house on a hill, bustling in preparation for the party, full of good things to eat, lovely things to wear, wonderful, expensive flowers to enjoy. The background is crammed with people to order about; the servants 'loved obeying'; friendly workmen swarm in the garden putting up a marquee; deliveries are made from shops; a band has been hired to put the finishing touches on the pleasures of the afternoon. The confident description is soaked in the values of middle-class authority as the genteel bourgeoisie prepares to play and enjoys every minute of the preparation. The pleasures at hand are both material and aesthetic, and even the perfect weather seems to endorse everything the Sheridans stand for. But the narration, insidiously, also undercuts its own exuberance with irony. Here, for example, is one of the daughters, Jose, practising for the display of her musical talents at the party:

> *Pom!* Ta-ta-ta *Tee*-ta! The piano burst out so passionately that Jose's face changed. She clasped her hands. She looked mournfully and enigmatically at her mother and Laura as they came in.

This Life is *Wee*-ary,
A Tear–a Sigh.
A Love that *Chan*-ges,
   This Life is *Wee*-ary,
A Tear–a Sigh.
A Love that *Chan*-ges,
   And then . . . Good-bye!

But at the word 'Good-bye,' and although the piano sounded more desperate than ever, her face broke into a brilliant, dreadfully unsympathetic smile.

'Aren't I in good voice, mummy?' she beamed.[39]

Katherine Mansfield mocks Jose's 'female accomplishments' in the same ironic manner and for the same reasons as Jane Austen does in *Pride and Prejudice*. Just as Mary bored the company in 1813, displaying her vanity rather than her love for music, so Jose produces the same eminently false effect in 'The Garden Party' of 1921. It is something of a shock to recognise the same device working so effectively in this twentieth-century story. Katherine Mansfield's attack on the inadequacy of the education of 'the daughters of educated men' is deepened by the story's account of the suffering taking place in the workmen's cottages just below the Sheridans' privileged hill. The false sentiment of Jose's song echoes the emotional disaster near at hand. The worker's world, which 'mummy' does not fully recognise (though the story emphasises the fact that she and her children live by and through their control of that world), is the scene of a casual tragedy. A workman has been killed in an accident; the news arrives during the preparations for the party. And the question of what is to be done in response to the news arises for only one character.

The character is Laura, a vaguely mutinous Sheridan daughter who, in the course of the story, acts as an intermediary between the two worlds – that of privilege and gaiety, and that of hardship, death and sorrow – and in the process is forced, if only momentarily, into the role of outsider.

We see Laura first in that most typical of middle-class occupations–romantic identification with an idealised working class. Laura, 'who loved having to arrange things', is assigned to direct the workmen who erect the marquee. Actually she directs nothing; the workmen know their job and choose the best site for the marquee in spite of her alternative suggestions. Laura's class loyalties vie with her sense of adventure; as she deals with the men their ease finally overcomes her slightly wounded dignity when they do not treat her with the deference afforded to a middle-class matron. Looking over the plan the foreman has hastily drawn, Laura dips her toe into rebellion:

> Oh, how extraordinarily nice workmen were, she thought. Why couldn't she have workmen for friends rather than the silly boys she danced with and who came to Sunday night supper . . . It's all the fault, she decided . . . of these absurd class distinctions. Well, for her part, she didn't feel them. Not a bit, not an atom . . . Just to prove how happy she was, just to show the tall fellow how at home she felt, and how she despised stupid conventions, Laura took a big bite out of her bread-and-butter as she stared at the little drawing. She felt just like a work-girl. [40]

This is, of course, transparent affectation, but it is also a potentially significant masquerade, small as the gesture of taking a bite of bread-and-butter might be. What the significance might be is suggested when the news of the death reaches the Sheridans. Laura, still influenced by her thoughts about the workmen, wants to stop the party, but her mother simply cuts her off:

'You are being very absurd, Laura,' she said coldly.
'People like that don't expect sacrifices from us. And it's not
very sympathetic to spoil everyone's enjoyment as you're
doing now.'

'I don't understand,' said Laura, and she walked quickly
out of the room into her own bedroom.[41]

Several truths of unequal significance operate in this
passage. Death *cannot* be conquered by stopping a party.
Pleasure *is* rare enough to deserve protection. The
workers do *not* have any expectations. And Laura really
does have no idea what she is doing. (That her mother
damns herself and her class goes without saying, but at
the same time *any* life that paused with every death
would soon be unliveable).

Laura's knowledge of the workmen is almost non-
existent. Their lane was forbidden territory in her
childhood and since she has 'grown up' she has only
walked through it once with her brother (and *alter ego*),
Laurie. On the walk she sees the lane as 'disgusting and
sordid. They came out with a shudder. But still one must
go everywhere; one must see everything.'[42] Laura in no
way connects herself with the lane. But this distanced
social voyeurism turns into something very immediate
with the news of the death, and just for a moment, at the
centre of the story, Laura steps outside her class and
circumstances into a confrontation with the equality of
all humanity in the face of mortality. What Laura 'sees'
at this point is far more important than what she has
'seen' during her educational tour of a working-class
habitat. For a moment, the social vocabulary of her tribe
fills Laura with disgust.

But only for a moment. What draws Laura back from
the isolation of her response to death is another
confrontation, this time with her own face framed by a
lovely hat that itself is the image of the pleasures of life

that only youth and privilege provide. What she sees in a mirror, walking away from her mother, is her identity:

> the first thing she saw was this charming girl in the mirror, in her black hat trimmed with gold daisies and a long black velvet ribbon. Never had she imagined she could look like that. Is mother right? she thought. And now she hoped that her mother was right.[43]

It is an extraordinary moment of conscience callousing over, with the lovely black hat repeating the colour of death. Katherine Mansfield's characteristic attention to detail allows her to conflate conscience and consciousness, beauty and vanity, bodily and mental satisfaction as Laura's politics turn on a glimpse of herself in the mirror. Giving up her chance for a public display of her beauty would be sacrificial; Laura slips easily back into the frivolity of the garden-party. On the next page she is afraid of being 'teased' about even thinking of making her egalitarian gesture.

Since Laura's class complacency is safe and the party is over, Mrs Sheridan gives her daughter a lesson in 'proper' charity. She sends her to the dead man's cottage with scraps from the party. In her stunning hat, her mind filled with the delights of the party, Laura self-consciously walks into the cottage with her basket and into the ceremonies of death. The two social rituals – the celebrations of the rich family, and the solemnity of death for the poor one – stress the discontinuity of experience. The man's wife, huddled like some primitive wounded thing by the fire, looks up at Laura, 'Her face, puffed up, red, with swollen eyes and swollen lips, looked terrible'. Laura, ashamed and embarrassed, blunders into the room with the dead man, and as the corpse is exhibited to her with tender, ritualistic pride, her response remains in the aesthetic mode of the party:

'he was wonderful, beautiful', a 'marvel', much better, in fact, in terms of beauty than her hat for which she now blurts out an excuse. The reader must recall the earlier significance of the hat and all that it has meant for Laura's conscience to understand the meaning of that apology. The story ends with Laura's confusion as she tries to express her feelings to Laurie and the meaning she has drawn from this encounter with death.

'The Garden-Party' is radically inconclusive. It is especially interesting in its portrayal of simultaneous but opposing goods, and in its treatment of the confusion of motivations and principles in life as opposed to the clarity of abstract ideas. Katherine Mansfield stressed this aspect of the story in a letter to William Gerhardi:

> And yes, that is what I tried to convey in *The Garden Party*. The diversity of life and how we try to fit in everything, Death included. That is bewildering for a person of Laura's age. She feels things ought to happen differently. First one and then another. But life isn't like that. We haven't the ordering of it.[45]

Katherine Mansfield's writing does, however, impose an order. It rejects the one that Laura accepts when she allows her aesthetic and class assumptions to dominate her at the moment when another kind of response was available to her. Laura only tastes the solitude that is the main diet of the women in many other stories, but the easiness with which a character can be thrust from full membership of a community to absolute exile in an instant, and the way in which such exile depends upon individual consciousness, underscores Katherine Mansfield's insistence on the fragility of identity.

While Katherine Mansfield's portrayal of the relationship between the self and others is always bleak, her late stories, as well as her early ones, are often comic. As Claire ·Tomalin points out about 'The Daughters of the Late Colonel', this very funny story 'offers an almost flawless descripion of two sisters who have been rendered unfit for life: not entirely a laughing matter.' In turning themselves into perfect objects for their father's will, the two old ladies have denuded themselves of their own. As Tomalin goes on to say of the story, 'it is quite possible to enjoy its jokes about early twentieth-century womanhood and miss the devastating nature of what it is saying.'[46] The querulous, timid narration itself expresses the central experience of the daughters as they try to grope their way out from under their masks after the death of their father.

The title of 'The Daughters of the Late Colonel' gives the circumstances of the story away. The two women, Constantia and Josephine, have indeed been 'constant' to their rumbling old father. These two pathetic creatures have existed only in relation to him, have lived only as 'daughters' and never in their own right. When the Colonel is dead, the world slips its moorings for the women who have been so stripped of the capacity for independent action by their life-long deference that they are scarcely sane.

> 'Oh,' groaned poor Josephine aloud, 'we shouldn't have done it, Con!'
> And Constantia, pale as a lemon in all that blackness, said in a frightened whisper, 'Done what, Jug?'
> 'Let them bu-bury father like that,' said Josephine, breaking down and crying into her new, queer-smelling mourning handkerchief.
> 'But what else could we have done?' asked Constantia wonderingly. 'We couldn't have kept him, Jug – we couldn't have kept him unburied. At any rate, not in a flat that size.'
> Josephine blew her nose; the cab was dreadfully stuffy.

'I don't know,' she said forlornly, 'It is all so dreadful. I feel we ought to have tried to, just for a time at least. To make perfectly sure. One thing's certain' – and her tears sprang out again – 'father will never forgive us for this – never!'[47]

Like frightened birds kept too long in captivity the two sisters cannot even think of flying. At the conclusion of the story, as they try to speak to one another of the future and to tell truths unrelated to their father's rule, they falter.

A pause. Then Constantia said faintly, 'I can't say what I was going to say, Jug, because I've forgotten what it was . . . that I was going to say.'

Josephine was silent for a moment. She stared at a big cloud where the sun had been. The she replied shortly, 'I've forgotten too.'[48]

Like the lives they might have had but which are no longer even memories of possibilities lost, the very words that might mean freedom have lapsed; the two sisters fall into the sun-darkening silence that has been their women's portion all along. Inured in their father's house they will rot with his furniture. Freedom has atrophied with lack of use. The two old women will continue as victims of a father who denied them the right to live.

Katherine Mansfield was angered by accusations of 'cruelty' and 'sneering' in the story. As she explained, again to William Gerhardi, the story was meant 'to lead up to that last paragraph, when my two flowerless ones turned with that timid gesture, to the sun. "Perhaps *now* . . ." And after that, it seemed to me, they died as surely as Father was dead.'[49]

It is finally, this theme, the 'sunlessness' of women's lives, and perhaps all lives, that is the dominant impression left by Katherine Mansfield's late fiction. It is the fiction of catastrophe, with varieties of deprivation, unhappiness and despair in control of human consciousness which Katherine Mansfield is constantly pushing to the breaking-point. The most important impulses behind the writing are emotions of anger and pity, and in her late work Katherine Mansfield at times abandoned the emotional cynicism of modernism to compose stories which are pure outcry.

'Life of Ma Parker' is the best of these sketches of despair. As always, Katherine Mansfield provides a social base for her tale in the form of a 'literary gentleman' who is shown priding himself on his 'handling' of Ma Parker, his aged, cheap, exhausted char, whom he overworks and underpays, and then undermines with accusations of petty theft. As the story switches to Ma Parker's consciousness, the way the world looks changes completely. She has a kind heart and merely pities the man for his messes as her mind fingers the memories of her disastrous life. Her husband died young of his baker's trade leaving her with the six of their thirteen children who survived. Her daughters 'went wrong', her boys 'emigrimated', and her last remaining girl was thrown back on her hands after the death of her husband, bringing with her a frail grandson who has been the light of Ma Parker's life and whom she has just buried. The contrast of the extraordinary stoicism of the woman and the tenderness of her love for the fragile child is painfully moving:

> 'Gran! Gran!' Her little grandson stood on her lap in his button boots. He'd just come in from playing in the street.
> 'Look what a state you've made your gran's skirt into–you wicked boy!'
> But he put his arms round her neck and rubbed his cheek against hers.
> 'Gran, gi' us a penny!' he coaxed.
> 'Be off with you; Gran ain't got no pennies.'

'Yes you 'ave. Gi' us one!'

Already she was feeling for the old, squashed black leather purse.

'Well, what'll you give your gran?'

He gave a shy little laugh and pressed closer.

She felt his eyelid quiver against her cheek. 'I ain't got nothing,' he murmured . . . [50]

This battered old woman, as 'squashed' as the purse that has held so little, has in fact possessed riches, and has lost them all. Katherine Mansfield refuses to mitigate the pathos of memories, and the story turns on the last of the little boy's remembered words. The theme, 'I ain't got nothing', is picked up forcefully when Ma Parker, finally overcome by her grief at her loss, somnambulantly walks out of the flat into the cold street.

There was a wind like ice. People went flitting by, very fast; the men walked like scissors, the women trod like cats. And nobody knew–nobody cared. Even if she broke down, if at last, after all these years, she were to cry, she'd find herself in the lock-up as like as not. [51]

Images of hostility and threat – wind and ice and scissors and cats and prisons – provide the final exclusion, generated by a consciousness that is left with only its own incredible stoicism. There is nowhere even for Ma Parker to cry. The narrative swoops in and out of her vocabulary to a general outcry of desolation and deprivation.

Katherine Mansfield's reputation for most of this century – that of a delicate female stylist with a reassuring line in colonial nostalgia – is rightly being revised. Her stories instead demand to be read as unremittingly critical accounts of social injustice grounded in the pretence of a 'natural' psychological and biological order that is disproved by the experience of consciousness. Image and plot, symbol and idea – all the elements of her fiction function as protests against any ideology of fixture and certainty. Katherine Mansfield's general commentary on her age is couched in her exposition of, her imaging of, contemporary women's consciousness, and in a prose attuned to catch the form of that experience. She implicitly demands the right to see women and their lives as the particulars from which the general historical situation can be deduced. But her fiction goes beyond an attempt to 'reflect' the age in which she lived; it is a body of work that incites to revolt through its critical appraisal of the circumstances Katherine Mansfield sees and records.

Notes

Introduction: Katherine Mansfield: Reception and Reputation

1. For what is probably the best short account to date of Katherine Mansfield's narrative technique, see Clare Hanson, *Short Stories and Short Fictions, 1880–1980* (London: Macmillan, 1985), pp. 55–81.
2. *Women in Love* (1921; rpt. Harmondsworth, Middlesex: Penguin, 1960), p. 105.
3. This is still the case. For example, C.A. Hankin entitles her recent study *Katherine Mansfield and Her Confessional Stories* (London: Macmillan, 1983), before pursuing a psychological reading of the stories in relation to Katherine Mansfield's life. Hankin agrees with Conrad Aiken that Katherine Mansfield 'used the short story as the medium for undisguised confession' (p. ix). To take another example, Vincent O'Sullivan in the Introduction to his edition of *The Aloe* (Manchester: Carcanet, 1983), emphasises the idea that 'Almost every Mansfield story can be taken back to some point of origin in the details of her life . . . . Unlike the larger talents of many writers, Mansfield simply does not move into anything like "pure fiction" ' (p. 7).

4. Murry's influence continues. In a recent reissue of Katherine Mansfield's *Journal* by Constable in 1984, his original personal and editorial remarks are printed without comment.

5. *Katherine Mansfield: A Critical Study* (London: Oxford University Press, 1952), p. 3.

6. The debate about Katherine Mansfield's 'femininity' or lack of it, has been a mainstay of Katherine Mansfield criticism. H.E. Bates illustrates the level of this discussion in *The Modern Short Story: A Critical Study* (London: Thomas Nelson, 1941). He says that 'her art is essentially feminine .... the rhetoric is delicate and rippling; it reads easily; one skims over the surface. But the dangers of such a style are clear. There is the danger that the voice of the narrator may become confused, even though wrongly, with the voice of the character; and one feels in certain of Katherine Mansfield's stories that this has happened, and that the girlish, chattering voice is the voice of the writer thinly disguised. Then there is the danger of monotony—of becoming bored, as one does in life, by a voice talking constantly of itself and answering all its own questions before anyone else has a chance' (pp. 129–30). Frank O'Connor, in *The Lonely Voice: A Study of the Short Story* (London: Macmillan, 1963), judges Katherine Mansfield adversely on the grounds that 'Most of her work seems to me that of a clever, spoiled, malicious woman' (p. 130), and hints that some kind of sexual abnormality is the source of her art. The list could go on interminably; T.S. Eliot, André Maurois, Katherine Anne Porter, Sylvia Berkman and Christopher Isherwood are among those who discuss Katherine Mansfield in these terms.

7. *The Second Sex*, trans. H.M. Parshley (1953; rpt. Harmondsworth, Middlesex: Penguin, 1972), p. 720.

8. Ibid., p. 719.

9. Ibid., p. 720.

10. *A Literature of Their Own*, rev. edn. (London: Virago, 1982), p. 246.

11. Ibid., pp. 246–7, 247–8, 246.

12. Ibid., p. 247.

Chapter 1: Life, Letters and Journal

1. Sydney Janet Kaplan, 'Katherine Mansfield's "Passion for Technique" ', in *Women's Language and Style*, ed. D. Buttruff and E.L. Epstein, *Studies in Contemporary Language*, No. 1 (Akron, Ohio: University of Akron Press, 1978), p. 120.
2. Biographical information on Katherine Mansfield has been taken from: *The Journal of Katherine Mansfield*, ed. John Middleton Murry (London: Constable, 1954); *The Letters of Katherine Mansfield*, 2 vols, ed. John Middleton Murry (London: Constable, 1928); *Katherine Mansfield's Letters to John Middleton Murry, 1913–1922*, ed. John Middleton Murry (London: Constable, 1951); Antony Alpers, *The Life of Katherine Mansfield* (New York: Viking, 1980); John Middleton Murry, *Between Two Worlds* (London: Jonathan Cape, 1935); and Ida Constance Baker (L.M.), *Katherine Mansfield: The Memories of L.M.*, intro. and linking text by Georgina Joysmith (London: Michael Joseph, 1971).
3. *Journal*, p. 107.
4. 'Introduction' to Katherine Mansfield, *Short Stories* (London: Dent, 1983), p. xvi.
5. *The History of Sexuality*, vol. I, trans. Robert Hurley (London: Allen Lane, 1978), pp. 61, 35.
6. For example, in a letter to Murry of 13 October 1920 she writes: 'these people who are nuts on analysis seem to me to have no sub-conscious at all. They write to *prove*–not to tell the truth.' (*Letters to Murry*, p. 560.)
7. Katherine Mansfield, *The Letters and Journals of Katherine Mansfield*, ed. C.K. Stead (London: Allen Lane, 1977), p. 76. Letter to Beatrice Campbell dated May 1916.
8. For a general discussion of symbolist principles and practice, see Frank Kermode, *Romantic Image* (London: Routledge & Kegan Paul, 1957).
9. *Journal*, p. 195. Entry dated 27 January 1920.
10. *Letters to Murry*, p. 94. Letter dated 1917. Katherine Mansfield seems also to have persuaded her friends to perceive her as a 'masked' woman – the incidence of the word in contemporary descriptions of her is too frequent to be coincidental. Lytton Strachey, writing to Virginia Woolf, speaks of Katherine Mansfield's 'ugly impassive mask of a face' (cited in Alpers, *Life of Katherine Mansfield*,

p. 248); Lady Glenavy remembers her 'little expression-less mask of a face' (Lady Glenavy, *Today We Will Only Gossip* (London: Constable, 1964), p. 68; and Ottoline Morrell, in 1918, was puzzled by Katherine Mansfield's 'curious smooth unruffled face, like a Japanese mask', and more effusively in 1933, imagined Katherine Mansfield's answer if her spirit could be asked what she was like: 'she would inevitably have hidden her sensitive soul behind a mask. If she explained herself at all she would say "I was really a child." ' (Ottoline Morrell, *Ottoline at Garsington* (London: Faber & Faber, 1974), p. 236, and Ottoline Morrell, 'K.M.', in *Katherine Mansfield: An Exhibition, September–November 1973*, REEM Collection (Humanities Research Centre, University of Texas at Austin, 1975), p. 8.)

11. *Journal*, p. 205.
12. Two often-recorded comments are significant here: the first is from Katherine Mansfield in 1917 after seeing Virginia Woolf's story 'Kew Gardens': 'We have got the same job, Virginia, and it is really very curious and thrilling that we should, quite apart from each other, be after so very nearly the same thing. We are, you know; there's no denying it.' (*Letters*, vol. I, p. 80. Letter dated August 1917.) The second is from Woolf's diary where she records her reactions to hearing of Katherine Mansfield's death: 'When I began to write, it seemed to me there was no point in writing. Katherine wont read it. Katherine's my rival no longer . . . . And I was jealous of her writing—the only writing I have ever been jealous of.' (*The Diary of Virginia Woolf*, ed. Anne Olivier Bell and Andrew McNeillie, vol. II (London: The Hogarth Press, 1978), pp. 226–7. Entry dated January 1923.)
13. *Journal*, pp. 202–3.
14. Ibid., p. 3.
15. Ibid., pp. 3, 9, 21. Entries dated 1906, 1907 and 1 October 1907.
16. Ibid., pp. 36–7. Entry dated May 1908. A letter from Edward Marsh to Rupert Brooke contains the following anecdote about Katherine Mansfield's attitude to feminism: 'Katherine Tiger . . . got turned out of an omnibus the other day for calling a woman a whore. She really ought to remember she's a Lidy. The provocation was that the

woman said all suffragettes ought to be trampled to death by horses. K. tho' not a suffragette protested, and the woman said, "You with your painted lips". Rather a squalid little story.' (Cited in Clare Hanson and Andrew Gurr, *Katherine Mansfield* (London: Macmillan, 1981), p. 6.)

17. *Letters to Murry*, p. 4. Letter dated Summer 1913. See also Katherine Mansfield, *The Scrapbook of Katherine Mansfield*, ed. John Middleton Murry (London: Constable, 1939), p. 109. On money see particularly the exchanges of letters in *Letters to Murry*, pp. 424–82; and John Middleton Murry, *The Letters of John Middleton Murry to Katherine Mansfield*, ed. C.A. Hankin (London: Constable, 1983), pp. 237–79.
18. *Journal*, p. 259.
19. *Letters*, vol. I, p. 28.
20. Ibid., pp. 82–3. Letter dated 11 October 1917.
21. *Journal*, p. 237. From an unposted letter dated 1921.
22. *Letters*, vol. II, pp. 91–2. Letter to Richard Murry dated 3 February 1921.
23. Ibid., p. 94. Letter dated February 1921.
24. *Letters to Murry*, pp. 380–1. Letter dated 10 November 1919.
25. Ibid., pp. 392–3. Letter dated 16 November 1919.
26. *Journal*, p. 273. Entry dated 1921.
27. Ibid., p. 179. Entry dated 1919.
28. Ibid., p. 220. Entry dated 1920.
29. Ibid., p. 121. Entry dated 1917.
30. *Critical Inquiry*, vol. 2, no. 1 (1975), p. 77.

Chapter 2: The Early Stories

1. Hanson, *Short Stories and Short Fictions*, p. 55.
2. Pierre Macherey, *A Theory of Literary Production*, trans. Geoffrey Wall (London: Routledge & Kegan Paul, 1978), p. 91.
3. *Letters*, vol. I, p. 236. Letter dated July 1919.
4. *Collected Stories of Katherine Mansfield* (London: Constable, 1945), p. 524.
5. Ibid., p. 529.
6. Ibid., p. 766.
7. Ibid., p. 530.
8. Ibid., pp. 533, 534.

9. Ibid., p. 549.
10. Ibid., p. 553.
11. Ibid., pp. 554, 555.
12. Ibid., p. 558.
13. Ibid., p. 580.
14. Ibid., p. 582.
15. *Letters to Murry*, p. 467. Letter dated 2 February 1920.
16. Ibid., p. 477. Letter dated 12 February 1920.
17. Cited in Hankin, *Katherine Mansfield*, p. 211. Letter to J.B. Pinker dated 3 May 1922. From an MS in the Alexander Turnbull Library, Wellington, New Zealand.
18. Ibid., p. 211.
19. *Collected Stories*, pp. 725–6. The idea was perhaps borrowed from *The Journal of Marie Bashkirtseff* which Katherine Mansfield read with keen attention in 1907. Marie, the daughter of a wealthy Russian landowner, and an independent young woman who studied painting with immense seriousness before dying at an early age of tuberculosis, makes the following observation: 'I admire the happy ones who eagerly swallow strawberries without troubling themselves about the little worms that one is nearly sure to find in them.' (*Journal of Marie Bashkirtseff*, trans. Mathilde Blind (London: Cassell, 1890), p. 452.) Katherine Mansfield turns this comment to comic advantage.
20. Berkman, *Katherine Mansfield*, pp. 43, 44.
21. *Collected Stories*, pp. 720, 721, 723.
22. Ibid., pp. 724–5.
23. Ibid., pp. 742–3.
24. Ibid., p. 754.
25. Ibid., p. 757.
26. Ibid., pp. 772–3.
27. Ibid., pp. 776, 773.
28. Woolf, *A Room of One's Own* (1929; London: Granada, 1977); p. 85.

Chapter 3: 'Prelude'

1. *Letters to Murry*, p. 15.
2. Ibid., p. 26.

3. *Letters*, vol. I, pp. 83–4. Letter dated 11 October 1917.
4. *Journal*, p. 94.
5. 'Katherine Mansfield', in *Not Under Forty* (London: Cassell, 1936), pp. 152–3.
6. See Berkman, *Katherine Mansfield*, p. 13 for an account of the Wordsworthian aspects in Katherine Mansfield's writing.
7. *Letters and Journals*, ed. Stead, p. 229. Letter to Ida Baker dated 29 August 1921.
8. *Collected Stories*, p. 11.
9. Ibid., p. 13.
10. 'Katherine Mansfield', *The London Magazine*, 2, no. 9, December 1962, p. 46.
11. *Collected Stories*, p. 17.
12. Ibid., p. 23.
13. Ibid., p. 46.
14. Ibid., p. 47.
15. Ibid., p. 34.
16. Ibid., p. 11.
17. Ibid., pp. 19, 23, 25.
18. Ibid., p. 24.
19. Ibid., pp. 27–8.
20. Ibid., pp. 53–4.
21. Ibid., p. 17.
22. Ibid., p. 54.

Chapter 4: Late Fiction

1. *Letters*, vol. II, p. 160. Letter dated 5 December 1921.
2. *Letters to Murry*, p. 467. Letter dated 3 February 1918.
3. Ibid., pp. 160–1, 163.
4. Both C.A. Hankin and Antony Alpers point out that the version of '*Je ne parle pas français*' that became the standard text was subject to editorial excisions that Katherine Mansfield only sanctioned reluctantly. While the inclusion of the discarded parts do help to clarify the story, its significance remains intact in the cut version. See Hankin, *Katherine Mansfield*, pp. 156–63; and Alpers, *Life of Katherine Mansfield*, pp. 270–3.
5. *Collected Stories*, p. 65.

6. Ibid., p. 67.
7. Ibid., p. 72.
8. Ibid., p. 80.
9. Ibid., p. 87.
10. Ibid., p. 88.
11. Ibid., p. 90.
12. See *Letters to Murry*, pp. 154-6. Letter dated 6 February 1918.
13. Ibid., p. 565. Letter dated 17 October 1920.
14. Ibid., p. 620. Letter dated December 1920.
15. *The Sexual Fix* (London: Macmillan, 1982), p. 3. For other important recent work on the construction of women's sexual desire, see Foucault, *The History of Sexuality*, and Ann Snitow *et al.*, *Desire: The Politics of Sexuality* (London: Virago, 1984).
16. *Collected Stories*, p. 96.
17. Ibid., p. 92.
18. Ibid., p. 96.
19. See Hankin, *Katherine Mansfield*, pp. 144-5.
20. *Collected Stories*, p. 102.
21. Ibid., p. 105.
22. *Letters*, vol. II, p. 89. Letter to Richard Murry dated 17 January 1921. See also Katherine Mansfield's review of Gertrude Stein's *Three Lives* in terms of the musicality of the prose in Katherine Mansfield, *Novels and Novelists* (London: Constable, 1930), pp. 273-4.
23. See, for example, Berkman, *Katherine Mansfield*, pp. 161-3.
24. *Collected Stories*, p. 331.
25. Ibid., p. 335.
26. Ibid., p. 336.
27. *Letters to Murry*, p. 671. Letter dated 13 October 1922.
28. See Hankin, *Katherine Mansfield*, pp. 226-7.
29. *Collected Stories*, pp. 212-3.
30. Ibid., pp. 236-7.
31. Ibid., p. 237.
32. Ibid., pp. 58-9.
33. Ibid., pp. 218, 220, 245.
34. Ibid., p. 396.
35. Ibid., p. 399.
36. Ibid., p. 393.
37. Ibid., p. 394.
38. Ibid., p. 401.

39. Ibid., p. 251.
40. Ibid., pp. 248–9.
41. Ibid., pp. 255–6.
42. Ibid., p. 256.
43. Ibid., p. 256.
44. Ibid., p. 260.
45. *Letters*, vol. II, p. 196. Letter dated 13 March 1922.
46. 'Introduction' to *Short Stories*, pp. xxiv–xxv.
47. *Collected Stories*, p. 269.
48. Ibid, p. 285.
49. Letters, vol. II, p. 120. Letter dated 23 June 1921.
50. *Collected Stories*, p. 302.
51. Ibid., p. 308.

Selected Bibliography

Books by Katherine Mansfield

The Aloe: with Prelude, ed. Vincent O'Sullivan (Manchester; Carcanet, 1983).

Collected Stories of Katherine Mansfield (London: Constable, 1945).

Four Poems, intro. Jeffrey Meyers (London: Eric and Joan Stevens, 1980).

Journal of Katherine Mansfield, ed. John Middleton Murry (London: Constable, 1954).

Katherine Mansfield's Letters to John Middleton Murry: 1913–1922, ed. John Middleton Murry (London: Constable, 1951).

The Letters and Journals of Katherine Mansfield: A Selection, ed. C.K. Stead (London: Allen Lane, 1977).

The Letters of Katherine Mansfield, ed. John Middleton Murry, 2 vols. (London: Constable, 1928).

Novels and Novelists, ed. John Middleton Murry (London: Constable, 1920).

Poems (London: Constable, 1923).

The Scrapbook of Katherine Mansfield, ed. John Middleton Murry (London: Constable, 1939).

Undiscovered Country: The New Zealand Stories of Katherine Mansfield, ed. Ian A. Gordon (London: Longmans, 1974).

The Urewera Notebook, ed. Ian A. Gordon (Oxford: Oxford University Press, 1978).

Biography, Criticism and Background Reading

· *Katherine Mansfield: An Exhibition, September–November 1973*, REEM Collection (Humanities Research Centre, University of Texas at Austin, 1975).

Katherine Mansfield Special Issue. Modern Fiction Studies, vol. 24, no. 3 (Autumn 1978).

Abel, Elizabeth (ed.), *Writing and Sexual Difference* (Brighton, Sussex: Harvester, 1982).

Allen, Walter, 'Katherine Mansfield', *The Short Story in English* (Oxford: Oxford University Press, 1981), pp. 165–75.

Alpers, Antony, *Katherine Mansfield* (London: Jonathan Cape, 1954).

——*The Life of Katherine Mansfield* (New York): Viking Press, 1980).

Arendt, Hannah, *The Origins of Totalitarianism* (New York: World Publishing, 1958).

Baker, Ida Constance, (L. M.), *Katherine Mansfield: The Memories of L. M.*, intro. Georgina Joysmith (London: Michael Joseph, 1971).

Bashkirtseff, Marie, *The Journal of Marie Bashkirtseff*, 2 vols, trans. Mathilde Blind (London: Cassell, 1890).

Bates, H. E., *The Modern Short Story: A Critical Survey* (London: Thoms Nelson, 1941).

Beachcroft, T. O., *The English Short Story*, vol II. Writers and Their Work Series, no. 169 (London: Longmans, 1964).

—— *The Modest Art: A Survey of the Short Story in English* (London: Oxford University Press, 1968).

Beauvoir, Simone de, *The Second Sex*, trans. H. M.

Parshley (1953; Harmondsworth, Middlesex: Penguin, 1972).

Berkman, Sylvia, *Katherine Mansfield: A Critical Study* (London: Oxford University Press, 1952).

Bowen, Elizabeth, 'A Living Writer', *Cornhill*, no. 1010 (Winter 1956/57), pp. 119–34.

Brophy, Brigid, 'Katherine Mansfield', *The London Magazine*, vol. 2, No. 9 (December 1962), pp. 41–7.

Carco, Francis, *Souvenirs Sur Katherine Mansfield* (Paris: Le Divan, 1934).

Carswell, John, *Lives and Letters: A. R. Orage, Beatrice Hastings, Katherine Mansfield, John Middleton Murry, S. S. Koteliansky*: 1906–1957 (London: Faber & Faber, 1978).

Carter, Angela, 'The Life of Katherine Mansfield', *Nothing Sacred* (London: Virago, 1982), pp. 158–61.

Cather, Willa, 'Katherine Mansfield', *Not Under Forty* (London: Cassell, 1936), pp. 139–66.

Daiches, David, 'Katherine Mansfield and the Search for Truth', *The Novel and the Modern World* (Chicago: University of Chicago Press, 1939), pp. 65–79.

Daly, Saralyn R., *Katherine Mansfield*. Twayne's English Authors Series (New York: Twayne, 1965).

Ellmann, Richard and Feidelson, Charles, Jr, *The Modern Tradition: The Backgrounds of Modern Literature* (New York: Oxford University Press, 1965).

Foot, John, *The Edwardianism of Katherine Mansfield* (Wellington, New Zealand: Brentwood's Press, 1969).

Foucault, Michel, *The History of Sexuality*, vol. 1, trans. Robert Hurley (London: Allen Lane, 1978).

Friis, Anne, *Katherine Mansfield: Life and Stories* (Copenhagen: Einar Munksgaard, 1946).

Glenavy, Lady Beatrice, *'Today We Will Only Gossip'* (London: Constable, 1964).

Gordon, Ian A., *Katherine Mansfield*. Writers and Their Work Series, no. 49 (London: Longmans, 1954).

Gurr, Andrew, *Writers in Exile: The Literary Identity of Home in Modern Literature* (Brighton, Sussex: Harvester, 1981).

Selected Bibliography

Hankin, C. A., *Katherine Mansfield and Her Confessional Stories* (London: Macmillan, 1983).

Hanson, Clare, *Short Stories and Short Fictions, 1880–1980* (London: Macmillan, 1985).

Hanson, Clare and Gurr, Andrew, *Katherine Mansfield* (London: Macmillan, 1981).

Hayman, Ronald, *Literature and Living: A Consideration of Katherine Mansfield and Virginia Woolf*. Covent Garden Eassys, no. 3 (London: Covent Garden Press, 1972).

Heath, Stephen, *The Sexual Fix* (London: Macmillan, 1982).

Hormasji, Nariman, *Katherine Mansfield: An Appraisal* (London: Collins, 1967).

Isherwood, Christopher, 'Katherine Mansfield', *Exhumations: Stories, Articles, Verses* (London: Methuen, 1966), pp. 64–72.

Kaplan, Sydney Janet, 'Katherine Mansfield's "Passion for Technique" ' *Women's Language and Style*, ed. Douglas Buttruff and Edmund L. Epstein. Studies in Contemporary Language, no. 1 (Akron, Ohio; University of Akron, 1978), pp. 119–31.

Kermode, Frank, *Romantic Image* (London: Routledge & Kegan Paul, 1957).

Kolodny, Annette, 'A Map for Rereading; Or, Gender and the Interpretation of Literary Texts', *New Literary History*, vol. 3 (1980), pp. 451–67.

——'Some Notes on Defining a "Feminist Literary Criticism" ', *Critical Inquiry*, vol. 2, no. 1 (1975), pp. 75–92.

Lawler, P. A., *The Loneliness of Katherine Mansfield* (Wellington, New Zealand: Beltane Book Bureau, 1950).

Lawrence, D. H., *Women in Love* (1921; Harmondsworth, Middlesex: Penguin, 1960).

Lawrence, Frieda, *'Not I, But the Wind . . . '* (London: Heinemann, 1935).

Lea, F. A., *The Life of John Middleton Murry* (London: Methuen, 1959).

Macherey, Pierre, *A Theory of Literary Production*, trans. Geoffrey Wall (London: Routledge & Kegan Paul), 1978.

Magalaner, Marvin, *The Fiction of Katherine Mansfield*. Crosscurrents Modern Critiques Series (London: Feffer & Simons, 1971).

Mantz, Ruth and Murry, John Middleton, *The Life of Katherine Mansfield* (London: Constable, 1933).

Marks, Elaine and de Courtivron, Isabelle (eds), *New French Feminisms* (Brighton, Sussex: Harvester, 1981).

Maurois, André, 'Katherine Mansfield', *Prophets and Poets*, trans. Hamish Miles (1935; Port Washington, New York: Kennikat Press, 1968).

Meyers, Jeffrey, *Katherine Mansfield: A Biography* (London: Hamish Hamilton, 1978).

Mitchell, Juliet and Rose, Jacqueline (eds), *Feminine Sexuality: Jacques Lacan and the école freudienne*, trans. Jacqueline Rose (London: Macmillan, 1982).

Moore, James. *Gurdjieff and Mansfield* (London: Routledge & Kegan Paul, 1980).

Morrell, Ottoline, *Ottoline at Garsington: Memoirs of Lady Ottoline Morrell: 1915–1918*, ed. Robert Gathorne-Hardy (London: Faber & Faber, 1974).

Murry, John Middleton, *Between Two Worlds: An Auto-biography* (London: Jonathan Cape, 1935).

—— *D.H. Lawrence: Son of Woman* (London: Jonathan Cape, 1931).

—— *Katherine Mansfield and Other Literary Portraits* (London: Peter Nevill, 1949).

—— *Katherine Mansfield and Other Literary Studies*, Foreword by T.S. Eliot (London: Constable, 1959).

—— *The Letters of John Middleton Murry to Katherine Mansfield*, ed. C.A. Hankin (London: Constable, 1983).

O'Connor, Frank, *The Lonely Voice: A Study of the Short Story* (London: Macmillan, 1963).

O'Sullivan, Vincent, *Katherine Mansfield's New Zealand* (London: Frederick Muller, 1975).

Pritchett, V.S., 'Books in General', review of *Collected Stories of Katherine Mansfield*. *The New Statesman and Nation*, vol. XXXI, no. 780 (2 February 1946), p. 87.

Rohrberger, Mary H., *The Art of Katherine Mansfield* (Ann Arbor, Michigan: University Microfilms International, 1977).

Selver, Paul, *Orage and the New Circle: Reminiscences and Reflections* (London: Allen & Unwin, 1959).

Showalter, Elaine, *A Literature of Their Own: British Women Novelists from Brontë to Lessing*, Rev. edn. (London: Virago, 1982).

Snitow, Ann, *et al.*, *Desire: The Politics of Sexuality* (London: Virago, 1984).

Tomalin, Claire, 'Introduction', *Katherine Mansfield, Short Stories* (London: Dent, 1983), pp. vii-xxx.

Walsh, William, *A Manifold Voice: Studies in Commonwealth Literature* (London: Chatto & Windus, 1970).

Willey, Margaret, *Three Women Diarists*. Writers and Their Work Series, No. 173 (London: Longmans, 1964).

Woolf, Leonard, *Beginning Again: An Autobiography of the Years 1911-1918* (London: The Hogarth Press, 1964).

Woolf, Virginia, *The Diary of Virginia Woolf*, ed. Anne Olivier Bell and Andrew McNeillie, vols. I-III. (London: The Hogarth Press, 1977, 1978, 1980).

—— *The Letters of Virginia Woolf*. ed. Nigel Nicolson and Joanne Traumann, vols. II-IV (London: The Hogarth Press, 1976, 1977, 1978).

—— *A Room of One's Own* (1929; London: Granada, 1977).

Index

144

Index